THE TRAINING OF NOH ACTORS

AND

THE DOVE

Mask: A Release of Acting Resources

A series of books written and illustrated by David Griffiths

This book is part of a series. The publisher will accept continuation orders which may be cancelled at any time and which provide for automatic billing and shipping of each title in the series upon publication. Please write for details.

THE TRAINING OF NOH ACTORS

AND

THE DOVE

Written and illustrated
by
David Griffiths

harwood academic publishers
Australia • Canada • China • France • Germany • India
Japan • Luxembourg • Malaysia • The Netherlands • Russia
Singapore • Switzerland • Thailand • United Kingdom

Amsteldijk 166
1st Floor
1079 LH Amsterdam
The Netherlands

British Library Cataloguing in Publication Data

Griffiths, David
  The training of noh actors; and, The dove. – (Mask: a release of
  acting resources; v. 2)
  1. No 2. Acting 3. Masques 4. English drama – 20th century
  I. Title II. The dove
  792'.028

  ISBN 3-7186-5716-3

Applications for permission to perform *The Dove* should be addressed to David Griffiths, Quaker Cottage, Quakers Lane, Rawdon, Leeds, LS19 6HU, England.

Cover illustrations by David Griffiths.

I dedicate this book to my late parents Jack and Doris,
who initiated and inspired the opportunity,
and to Vicky who supported me unselfishly throughout the period of
research and writing, and shared the joy of its completion.

CONTENTS

INTRODUCTION TO THE SERIES

Mask: A Release of Acting Resources is a fully illustrated four-volume series, which examines the effect of mask in performance.

This series reflects my practical work and draws upon my research into the secret world of the Noh of Japan and the Masquerade of Nigeria, the comic style of the Commedia Dell'Arte and the training of actors through mask in Britain.

The series also includes my three written masked plays called *The Dove, Please Be Gentle* and *Touch*, which transform and test the results of my experiments into theatrical practicality.

David Griffiths

ACKNOWLEDGEMENTS

I would like to thank the following: Dr David Richards for sowing the seed and making the original research enquiry on my behalf; the School of English, University of Leeds, for giving me the opportunity; the British Academy for setting the precedent of offering me an annual award and having faith that it would be used responsibly; Tom Needham for his friendship and his "investment" of £1000, without which I would not have been able to visit Japan; the Society of Friends for their grant of £500, which was given to me at a time great financial need; all those at the Tramshed in Glasgow who led me to *The Mahabharata* and Peter Brook; Chris and Vayu Banfield who have have embraced me with a continuous stream of encouragement, practical help and invaluable advice; Alan Vaughan Williams, a wonderfully exciting theatre director, who gave me some of my early directing work and who continues to support and encourage without qualification; and Professor Martin Banham who supervised and guided me through my original enquiry with extreme care, the right amount of humour and encouraging portions of excitement.

In Japan, I am eternally grateful for the extraordinary hospitality and kindness given to me by my supervisor Professor Yasunari Takahashi, Jo Barnett CBE (Director of the British Council, Tokyo) and his staff at Kyoto, Chizuko and Naoichi Tsuyama my hosts and dear friends, Richard Emmert, and Fumiye Miho and Friends at the Friends' House in Tokyo.

LIST OF ILLUSTRATIONS

INTRODUCTION

The artistic philosophy, the professional administration, the quality of training and performance still to be found in the masked Noh Theatre of Japan, satisfies much of the criteria which I demand for professional theatre in the West. This blueprint seemingly matches that which exists for dance and music, the two performing arts I cite in Volume 1 as having those basic qualities of training, repertoire and performance experience, which lead to standards of excellence rarely found in the theatre.

Definition – NOH: The Discipline of Accomplishment

I embarked upon an exploration of theory and fact gleaned from a four month visit to Japan as a research scholar at Tokyo University, in order to verify – or otherwise – this general supposition.

I base my enquiry mainly upon the observations and experiences I made whilst attending rehearsals for, and the subsequent performances of, Noh plays performed by the major Noh companies in Tokyo and Kyoto: I spent much of my time observing the main actors of the Kanze school. I was also able to collate much academic criticism and research material drawn from publications and papers written by Japanese scholars of Noh, recently translated into English.

Throughout this book my perspective remains focussed upon the training and performing art of the Noh actor and the plays and arenas in which they are performed.

The distinctive style of Noh, which has survived and been supported by over six centuries of succeeding performers and audiences, maintains a clearly defined philosophical base and mirrors many elements inherent in the Japanese psyche: namely, an immediately recognisable sense of self-discipline, a dramatic sense of dignity and grace, an unnerving strength and virtuosity accompanied by open displays of ritualistic humility.

I shall consider the influences of music, rhythm and dance, costumes, properties, and the special physical proportions and qualities of the Noh stage and auditorium which reflect many architectural features embodied in shrines and temples (see ill. 1); the repertoire of plays, their form, and how all these elements combine to influence the detail of the Noh actor's training and preparation.

1. Kukujudai. Eikando Temple, Kyoto

Whilst offering a brief history of the development of Noh from the days of Kan'ami to the present day, I shall continually refer to ways in which the 'families' of performers and assistants developed skills, which seemed to serve them so well, ensuring that Noh survived the rigorous scrutiny of audiences and patrons; an inbuilt survival kit which sustained a continuing patronage through some of the most devastating physical and spiritual disasters in world history.

It is interesting to note that at the end of this 20th century the Noh actor has never been so financially and artistically secure. I am convinced that the continuing interest in Noh in Japan, and the level of support it continues to receive, is largely due to the sustained quality of the training of the performers and their art.

1

A BRIEF HISTORY OF NOH

Kan'ami and Zeami to the Present Day

Noh theatre as it is experienced today, has a lineage which is directly linked to Kiyotsugu Kan'ami (1332–1386) and his son Motokiyu Zeami (1363–1443). Both were Buddhists and deeply religious. The plays and the theatre form they created, contained much in the way of symbols and imagery, and could be directly linked to Shinto principles.

Their work also revealed a powerful link with the natural and supernatural. All the masked characters represented ghosts which were both ordinary and demonic, real and imagined.

What were the influences which seemed to crystalise into this refined, highly stylised dramatic form, in the hands of Kan'ami and Zeami at this particular time in Japanese history, and what was the essential ingredient which was to allow it to remain almost unaltered in its form of unbroken presentation for the ensuing six hundred years?

Like the emergence of the genius of Shakespeare at the end of a period of medieval experiment by many writers, the Sarugaku-Noh as it was called – a form of masked dance drama which also included in its programme a set of comic anecdotes, written and 'rehearsed' by Kan'ami – 'emerged', and seemed to captivate and engage the sustained patronage of the shogunate of the period.

Where had it come from?

The natural environment often provokes active engagement in corporate worship, the content of which links the basic ingredients of fear and respect by those who wish to survive in harmony with the elements and the landscape. Certainly a form of ritual celebration, central to most dramas, could be traced to the festivals surrounding the seasons, the planting and harvesting of essential crops.

These celebrations and rituals would be held in special places and would be central to the cyclic order of the universe as experienced in the clearly defined seasonal changes. They would bring together the community, and would be prepared for and 'performed' with an appropriate sense of occasion.

There were also forms of worship at holy places in which corporate communion would take place at regular intervals, and from which ritual dances, rites, and pantomimes called *Kagura* evolved. Strictly speaking

Kagura means God music, though it became more generally understood to be Shinto music and the rites associated with it.

There was also a strong influence from the differing cultures of China and Asia in the Nara and Heian periods of the seventh century. Dancing and music forms such as *Bugaku* and *Gigaku*, and acrobatic and mime narratives called *Dengaku* and *Sangaku* were introduced and popularised at court. These 'entertainments' brought with them ornate and beautifully fashioned costumes and masks.

As the centuries evolved and there was a fusion of what was native and what was imported, both the Shinto and Buddhist religions encouraged the presentation of their philosophy and faith, through a new dramatic narrative form presented by an assortment of troupes of performers who had become 'attached' to their shrines and temples. In a way, a parallel can be made during the same period with the more accessible medieval Miracle Cycles and Mystery plays which were establishing themselves in Britain.

By the time Kan'ami and his professional 'family' troupe of players had established their art and sustained a livelihood, narrative elements in the *Sarugaku* had developed and shifted the emphasis of the form of presentation in performance, and the *Sarugaku-Noh* had arrived.

In 1374 the Shogun, Ashikaga Yoshimitsu, whilst attending a performance of Kan'ami and his troupe, at the Imakumano Shrine in Kyoto, decided there and then that the new form of Sarugaku-Noh which he was seeing for the first time was so enchanting that he instantly adopted the troupe that performed it and became its patron.

Over the next few years, he took a special interest in fostering the intellectual, artistic and social development of Kan'ami's son Zeami, exposing him to the learnéd attentions of poets and philosophers. Such a comprehensive education was unusual because of the traditionally lowly social status of the performer. But it is clear that this period in Zeami's development was fundamental in its influence upon the refined form of Noh which was to emerge when he eventually became the young master of the Kanze school on the death of his father in 1386.

The evidence which accompanies this short history of the origins of Noh is open to much conjecture. The facts are few and to some extent are not unlike the kind of developments which were being experienced elsewhere in Europe.

However, the most influential and crucial documents which were compiled and completed towards the end of his life, and was left for future generations of Noh actors to study and follow, were the *Treatises of Zeami*: twenty-one major statements on the art of Japanese Noh theatre. In my view, this is one of the most important and yet most neglected documents on actor-training that has ever been written.

Before I address my attention to this vital document, in the next chapter, I wish to offer a detailed description of the physical shape and structure of the performance and preparation areas of the Noh stage, of how this space is filled with an assortment of performers, and finally offer a detailed examination of the composition of a Noh play in all its constituent parts.

The Origins of the Noh Stage

The Noh acting space is simply defined as being an approximate nineteen foot square which is physically 'bridged' by an entrance corridor for the main performers, linking the 'dressing' space to the up stage right corner of the acting square. The audience surrounds two, and sometimes three, sides of this square, thus creating a 'thrust' arena.

The design of this simple space evolved over many years, but had become more or less fixed, as described above, by the latter half of the sixteenth century. It is a straightforward matter to trace its shape and scale to the 'gathering' space in which celebratory dances and narratives were conducted outdoors, in the natural landscape, within convenient proximity to the community dwellings.

Performers must be seen and heard. The exterior acoustic defines its own limitations for the performer. Gatherings outside seem to have a more embracing sense of contact when the performing space is enclosed within the defined outline of buildings or a garden.

Without exception, all the Noh theatre spaces which have been constructed in Japan possess this sense of intimacy. Audiences are measured in hundreds rather than thousands. Even the National Noh Theatre in Tokyo, despite its magnificent wooden stage and auditorium, is a performing space, where the actor seems always in close proximity to all the members of the audience.

In the early outdoor performances, the travelling troupes carried only the minimum of properties and staging. Essentially fit-up and temporary, it could be set in any reasonable landscape, and could be a system of stakes, ropes and tentage which would simply define the area for preparation, performance, and audience.

It is not difficult to assume that Masters such as Kan'ami, once he had secured reasonable financial support, would invest in such basic needs as a decent portable flooring which could reproduce in its size and surface the training and 'rehearsal' space in which the plays were prepared. The evolution and fixing of this performing space would naturally follow from these practical requirements. It is no surprise to actors who are continually performing that the performing area 'evolves' naturally once the basic shape and requirement of the drama has been defined.

As the troupes became more and more popular and associated with their patrons and therefore with the social and political development of Japan, so the programmes and place of performance seemed to require a more systemised style of presentation.

Noh stages became fixed in the sense that their basic design was constructed as a roofed building separated from the area (or building) where the

2. Origins of the Noh stage:
(a) A conjectural Noh stage at the time of Zeami
(b) Northern Noh stage at the Nishi Honganji, Kyoto (1591)

audience was seated, and linked to a preparing and dressing space by a corridor. The stage and corridor was raised above a 'garden' of gravel or sand which also filled the space between the 'auditorium' and the stage.

The earliest example of such a stage which is still in existence is the northern stage at the Nishi Honganji in Kyoto and dates from 1591 (see ill. 2(b)). Its design serves as the model upon which all subsequent Noh stages have been built, with few modifications.

The other links with its outdoor ancestry is embodied in the stylised painted pine and bamboo designs on the upstage walls, and by the three miniature pine trees which descend in height and perspective from the upstage right pillar, dividing equally the length of the bridge.

Occasionally paper pendants adorn the space between the pillars reminding us of the deep association with the Shintoism and the shrines where Noh is still performed as a religious ritual.

The greatest feature of the Noh stage is its simplicity. Even when it is set within the 'high-tech' concrete walls of a towering Tokyo cuboid, the scale and design of this simple performing space seems to carry with it its own, magical, uncluttered focus of pure beauty. As you enter, and join in the communion with the rest of the audience, you are aware of the wooden beams and thatch and open joints and carvings of craftsmen.

'On Funa-Benkai' National Noh Theatre May 2nd 1989.

3. *On Funa-Benkai*, National Noh Theatre, Tokyo

4. The rock garden of the Daisen-in Temple, Kyoto

Here is an immediate and continuing link with the constructing art of a previous age.

From the first invocations of the flute to the concluding exit of the musicians, this illusion of time suspended in the distant past is maintained. You remain, as you began, with the stage.

It is transformed in performance in time and place according to the words of the narrative. It is gilded only with the strokes of shapes and sounds and properties which allow the minimal interference with its basic worldliness. This stage is 'everywhere' in location and time.

Its definition is altered only by the skills of the performers, and is never tainted by over-elaborate sets and accompanying technological distortions of sound and light. A still, quiet, general light reproduces that of daylight for both performer and audience. The Noh theatre is a place for deep contemplation, and everything in its design supports and respects that philosophy.

The Noh Stage and its Occupants

The stage is made of Japanese Cypress (hinoki) and is highly polished, enabling the actors to perform in stockinged feet their characteristic 'gliding' movements which so heightens the gracefulness of their performance. The surface remains always in this highly polished, spotless state. Nothing is ever built onto it. It is a treasured surface that is raised to a height of about three feet above the base of the auditorium. All symbolic properties are light enough to be carried, being simple frameworks in bamboo, bound with cotton tape.

Suspended beneath the stage are a series of large open-necked ceramic jars, which act as sound resonators when the actors stamp their feet during the dance. This extraordinary resonance also seems to colour the texture of the vocal and instrumental voices.

There are specific 'areas' where the performers 'set' themselves. The 'acting' area is clearly defined by the square of cypress boarding which runs at right-angles from the front of the stage, down stage to upstage and ends at a line which forms the upstage line of the bridge. Behind this line the floorboards run from stage right to stage left.

Down stage of this area, on an imaginary line running from right to left, sit the four musicians who play stick drum, hip drum, shoulder drum and flute. There is enough room for each of these players to be able to spread themselves sufficiently to play their instruments unhampered by each other, and also leave enough room for attendants and actors to pass by the stick drummer and flautist with ease. The attendants sit below the upstage wall, upstage of the musicians and are usually tucked in line, into the upstage right corner.

At each corner of the acting square is a named pillar, determined by the performer who most often occupies the adjacent space. Thus the upstage right pillar is the Shite pillar, upstage left is the Flute pillar, and down stage left is the Waki pillar.

The remaining down stage right pillar is named after its practical use as a locating marker for the masked actor and is called the Sighting pillar. Perhaps it is appropriate at this point to define the main characters in the Noh play:

The *Shite* (the person who does) is the chief actor in the Noh and in most cases is masked.

The *Waki* (side) is unmasked and is the second most important actor after the Shite. He often acts as a foil for the Shite, and introduces sequences of action setting the scene. He is often unnamed, has no described personality and functions as an agent of the audience asking the kind of questions which they may ask of the action, and characters.

The *Tsure* assists, and usually acts as a companion character to the Shite and Waki. He is sometimes masked if he accompanies the Shite.

The Ai (between interval) is played by the *Kyogen* (outrageous language) actor who usually delivers monologues, reiterating the narrative of the play in a less complex linguistic style than the Shite. The same Kyogen actor, with his fellow actors, also performs the comic 'interludes' in an

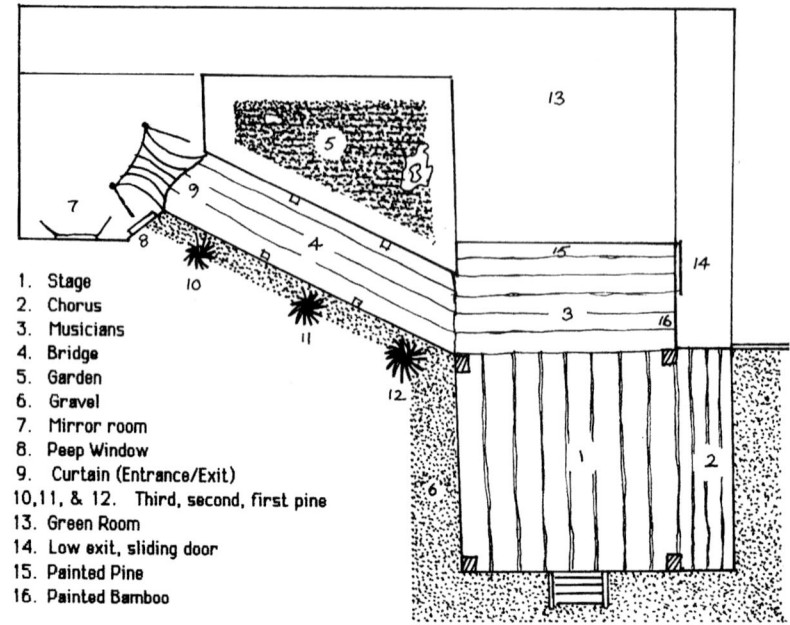

1. Stage
2. Chorus
3. Musicians
4. Bridge
5. Garden
6. Gravel
7. Mirror room
8. Peep Window
9. Curtain (Entrance/Exit)
10, 11, & 12. Third, second, first pine
13. Green Room
14. Low exit, sliding door
15. Painted Pine
16. Painted Bamboo

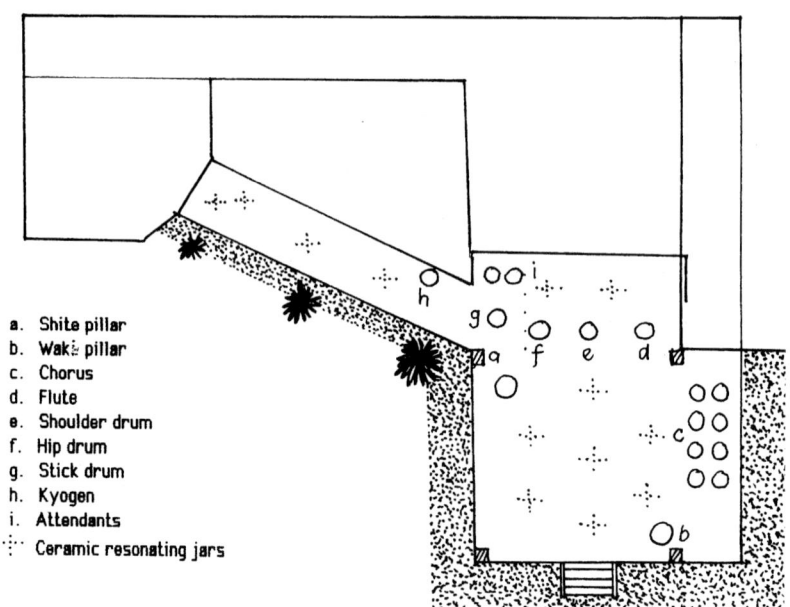

a. Shite pillar
b. Waki pillar
c. Chorus
d. Flute
e. Shoulder drum
f. Hip drum
g. Stick drum
h. Kyogen
i. Attendants
Ceramic resonating jars

5. The constituent parts of a Noh stage

evening's programme, which slot between Noh plays; their function being a kind of transitory release from the demands made by a Noh play upon the audience.

Finally, in a 'fenced' area stage left of the acting square, the width of two kneeling bodies, is the space set for the Chorus who are usually eight in number. They remain in a kneeling position during all the sequences which include the main actors, only leaving the stage with them during the Kyogen sequence. The chorus and musicians area is never used by the protagonists.

The down stage edge of the acting square is traditionally assumed to be facing North, though this is not necessarily so in modern Noh theatres as it depends upon how the stage is set architecturally within its concrete shell.

The bridge and stage are covered with an 'eaved' roof which in style resembles the thatched roofs adorning temples and shrines. The open horizontal beams stand at least ten feet above the stage, and all the cross-spars and joints between them are exposed.

In the far upstage left corner is a small sliding door which allows stooping access to actors or attendants during the performance, to and from the dressing rooms. Immediately above and down stage of this door is a stylised painting of a Bamboo plant, whilst the upstage wall is covered with the painting of a Pine. All the walls are panelled in cypress.

6. Kita School stage, Tokyo

7. Tessen-Kai Noh Laboratory, Tokyo

Entrance onto the bridge, from the dressing rooms is made through a light, five-coloured rolled curtain, which is raised by the simple action of lifting two poles attached to its lower end, and set the curtain's length away. Behind this curtain, and to its right, is the Mirror Room, the special place where the Shite prepares his mask and his character before his entrance. From the Mirror Room it is possible to see the stage from a peep window set in the wall down stage of the curtain.

Behind and between the sliding door and the Mirror Room, is the Dressing and Green rooms, in which there are no tables or chairs, just the traditional tatami matting and the sliding screened divisions.

This is a brief description of the permanent Noh performing and preparing space, the scale of which varies little, save for the length of the bridge as determined by the size of the cuboid (usually concrete!) which houses the theatre. Most auditoria are furnished with seats which are arranged to face the down stage and stage left facets of the acting area, and which are gently raked, although the Tessen-Kai Noh Laboratory – the home of a branch of the Kanze School in Tokyo – is fitted with Tatami matting on which the audience squats or kneels in familiar Japanese style. The acoustics of Noh theatres are almost one hundred per cent.

It is into this unchanging space that the performers create the masked, danced dramas; time and location being determined through simple references in the dialogue, by the arrangement of minimal, open-framed properties, and by the physical language of the dance. A particular time or place is 'located' just for the moment it is needed in the narrative, returning always to the basic, timeless space, and design.

The Constituent Parts of a Noh Play

It is not my intention to explain in detail the complex language of the Noh performance, but rather to provide a basic picture of how the composition of a Noh programme is presented, and to indicate the unique aura surrounding Noh in performance.

The Noh actor is heavily costumed. If he is a Shite, he is almost always masked, and all his movements are related directly to that mask. If he is a Waki, he is unmasked, although his movements, complement in style those of the masked Shite.

He (both Waki and Shite) chants rather than speaks his dialogue, which is usually highly stylised and in verse.

He 'dances' rather than strides about the acting space, adopting a highly specialised and technically difficult gliding motion to travel across the acting square. He performs many sequences of dialogue constructed like monologues, (the chant being taken over or continued by the chorus) and his sequential physical movements are meticulously choreographed.

He spends much of his time opening, closing and shaping a fan, which is regularly transferred to either hand and is his most articulate property. Indeed, a knowing audience will be looking particularly closely at his fan work to ascertain – in general terms – the worth of his technical skills.

Underlying all of this is a quality of grace and strength that comes from a basic posture, which is always in a controlled tension; a great energy source which the audience should not be able to see but be aware of. Something in the air.

Some performances are preceded by a short ritual, called Shi-Mai, presented in rehearsal kimono, where the Shite offers a simple, monologue and sequence of movement. They are supported vocally in the chant by two or three attendants who remain 'seated' in the positions usually occupied by the musicians. The Shi-Mai is a public display of humility by the Noh actor (after the shite) in taking on the mantle of the characters in the narrative which is about to unfold. For Grotowski it is almost 'sacrificial' (see *Acting through Mask.* p. 14).

An invocatory wailing played on the flute from behind the curtain Signals the beginning of the performance. This is then followed by the entrance of the musicians (see ill. 8) in correct order, a set distance apart, walking slowly in procession along the bridge to their respective positions. They are met by attendants who eventually help them to set themselves upon an unfolded stool.

From the sliding door upstage left emerge the members of the chorus, who settle in a kneeling position, in two rows of four, one behind the other. Each carries a fan which is placed before them, in line with their knees when they are not chanting, and is lifted and set vertically in the right hand, resting on the right knee when they are actively chanting.

Once the musicians are set, instruments tuned, attendants retired to their location, the flautist 'invokes' the Waki who enters along the bridge, makes a descriptive introduction describing his character, location and purpose, before settling within close proximity to his pillar, either on a drum-like seat, or in a one-legged squat.

The invocation signalling the entrance of the Shite is again given by the flautist. When he appears, he pauses close to the third pine to establish his character and his state, before finally settling close to his pillar and beginning the drama.

From this point onwards a seeming battle of will develops, where each element strives to dominate others as well as the emotional loyalty of their audience. It is to the emotions that the Noh drama is addressed. Sounds and rhythms, words and action are all projected into the performance 'space' for assimilation.

Sometimes phrases from the flute are clearly acknowledged and taken by the actors or chorus, and the pitch of the vocalising becomes framed within a regular spread of notes.

Sometimes the extraordinary, syncopated rhythms, accompanied by the owl-like screeches and hoots – the 'Yo-ho' factor – uttered and beaten out by the drummers seem to slice savagely across a pattern of movement or a unison choral response. The effect can be hypnotic.

Hip drum   Shoulder drum   Stick drum

Flute

8. Noh musicians and their instruments

It is from this whirlpool of will, with all its inbuilt stretching and bending of notes, phrasing, dance and the demand for attention, that the emotional energies are released, to the audience. And yet, paradoxically, the form rigidly adheres to a fixed and highly complex rhythmical notation, and an 'unseen' pattern of cuing.

Apart from what is done within the dance in terms of sound shapes and colours reflected in the narrative, the visual spectacle of costume and fan complementing the mask is what demands attention – if the actor is strong and skilled.

For most of his time on stage the actor (Shite) is either absolutely motionless, or dancing, at the sametime expounding his own condition by way of a monologue or occasional exchange with the Waki.

He will sometimes use a staff, sword or other small property, but he will always have a fan to hold and use. The fan can represent a receptacle for alms, a vessel to drink from, a screen to hide tears: mostly it is used as an extension of an arm, being opened and closed according to the shape of the dance. It is usually passed from one hand to the other, the 'empty' hand remaining shaped as though still holding the fan.

The many-layered costume covers the body and heavily disguises the actor, although there will always be an awareness of the way the body is held beneath the costume to support the distinctive gliding and spinning movements in performance. There is also something about the moulded structure of these costumes which helps the actor to determine the best, and sometimes the only way in which to display them.

The long rectangular kimono-style sleeves are folded, swung, tossed and suspended, according to the symbolic significance of the character's dance. Most of the masked Shite characters wear highly stylised wigs which complement the masks and costume, and which complete the 'properties' of the dance.

Many of the elaborate costumes have remained, like the masks, within the care of the families of the schools who use them. In my view, they have become one of the main physical links for the modern actor with generations of predecessors.

When they have become worn or damaged to an extent which dilutes their performance effectiveness they are replaced by exact replicas. Thus each generation of actor is confronted not only with the same character, but with all the physical and technical accoutrements which accompany and support its presentation on stage. This is the form and the presentation which the Noh audience expects to see.

In modern evenings of Noh, similar to those I experienced in Tokyo and Kyoto, the number of plays in an evening's cycle will number no more than two, and will be placed either side of a Kyogen.

A traditional Noh cycle, strictly speaking, would comprise five plays which are distinguished by type: God, Warriors, Women, Mad Women, and Demons and also their order of performance; one to five as cate-gorised by type.

This cycle would be broken up in sequence by four Kyogen 'inter-ludes.' It would conform to a Yo-Ha-Kyu principle which would deter-mine the order of the performance of the plays selected. So, categories and types are chosen to conform with the Yo-Ha-Kyu structure which will truly engage the spectator, developing in intensity as the cycle progresses.

Yo-Ha-Kyu quite simply follows an Introductory-Development-Con-clusion structure which supports the 'beginning, middle and end' for-mula of the traditional 'well made play' of western theatre. It is much more complex than this, but at this juncture will satisfy the general principle upon which the cycle of plays are chosen.

It is suggested that modern audiences are, in general, no longer able to 'stay' with a full cycle of five plays, thus the much reduced pro-gramme, although one suspects that the resources of performance would also be stretched in terms of numbers and the ability to sustain the required high level and intensity of performance skills.

So whilst the modern programmes focus upon the more energetic and spectacular of the plays, all categories are represented.

The Kyogen

The Kyogen, which parallels the Satyr play in the Greek festival, and the Intermezzi of the 15th and 16th century Italian theatre, acts as a form of comic relief and release for the audience, and is positioned in the programme between the Noh plays.

The stories are usually a Father and Son, Master and Servant affair where one is trying to outdo or undermine the credibility of the other. The language is usually lively and straight-forward, having little of the elevated style of a Noh play in content, although the dance movements and the vocal dexterity and intonation of the Kyogen actor still mirrors in technical skill that of the Noh. There are elements of burlesque in the repetitive exchanges between the characters as they quickly develop the plot using a more complex exchange of physical gymnastics and word patterns.

The actors of the Kyogen are usually unmasked although there are classic plays which demand the mask of Monkey or Fox. The costumes are more akin to the rehearsal clothes of Noh, save that they are more boldly printed and decorated. They also have wide shoulder-pads which distinguishes the overall shape of the Kyogen performer from his Shite/Waki counterpart.

The Kyogen stage is devoid of chorus and musicians, thus the Kyogen play relies more heavily upon the dual elements of speech and move-ment. The training for Shite and Kyogen actors in terms of technique is similar, and requires the same commitment, but it is clear that because of its 'simplicity' in form, and in terms of the few actors needed to perform, a Kyogen is much easier to transport, assemble and present than Noh – and is much cheaper also!

Perhaps it is also important at this juncture to remind ourselves of the Kyogen character who often occupies an important part in the composition of a number of Noh plays. His role is not comic but more in keeping with the elevated tone of the Noh play, although his language is more colloquial and accessible to the audience.

One final element in the performance of a Noh play is the presence of the stage attendants. Firstly it must be noted that the chorus members are made up of Shite performers or Shite in training. It is usually Shite who are not performing as chorus who act as attendants. Their main function is to attend to the need of the Shite; to keep a close watch on the state of their costume – adjusting the folds or ties or trailing flow if necessary – and add or subtract props as and when required.

It is interesting to note that one of the attendants often proves to be a very important and senior Shite, so that in case of an accident to a shite during the performance he can immediately take over the role.

When a prop has been finished with, it is simply discarded and left, being of no further use to the Shite. This is done during the action, openly, before the audience. The attendant will unobtrusively remove the prop and return to his 'attending' position or retire with it offstage,

9. Kyogen sequence, National Noh Theatre, Tokyo

usually through the sliding door upstage left. Sometimes, in certain plays a whole layer of clothing is removed, and wig changed, again without any attempt to conceal the fact from the audience.

What is surprising is that this 'openness' does not in any way reduce the impact of the transformation of character when revealed by the Shite as he turns to face the audience.

Such is the focus upon the skill of the Shite, and the configuration of music and chorus, that although the attendants perform their tasks quite openly, keeping the performing space clear of all discarded props in case they get in the way of the performers, they remain out of the mind's eye.

The attendants also are in a position where they act as onlookers to the action, contributing to it just by being focussed upon it, in attendance; another layer of silent chorus.

Each Noh performance is an event in itself. It will be performed at its location once only. There will be no anticipation or hope of a long 'run'. That is not to say that plays in a year's repertoire will not be repeated. Occasionally this will happen once or twice, even with the same assembly of performers, but only very rarely, and never in the same theatre.

I mention this because it is the uniqueness of each performance, having its solitary position in the calendar, which gives it a sense of occasion, a one-off celebration in the same way that an orchestral concert programme rarely is seen in the same concert-hall twice with the same performers.

10. Another Kyogen sequence

Which brings me briefly to the final constituent part of the Noh performance, the audience. Like attenders of music concerts in the west, many arrive armed with Noh score-texts which they follow assiduously throughout the performance. Some will be amateurs keen to follow the route of their professional mentors, for they will be pupils of actors in the major schools.

The rest will be devotees, and their attendance will be as significant as sharing an act of worship. For others, the Noh will be like going to the Opera or Ballet and will have similar social associations. Unlike western theatres in cities like London, there will be very few tourists in attendance. There are very few tourists in Japan!

Similarly to a concert audience, most will be familiar with the content of the programme and its performers, and will have come with the same expectancy of skilled professionalism. In my experience the level of attention is equally intense and concentrated. There is a sense in which all the familiar constituent parts re-form and regenerate a unique sense of novelty.

The emotional impact is intimate, reflective and meditative. One is lulled into a trance-like state of appreciation of the display of skills which produces such a variety of emotional response. The story-line is brief, and known. The audience have arrived to see HOW it is done.

Whilst they may go away disenchanted by the interpretation, they rarely depart without the recognition of the high standard of performance skills they have witnessed. Like all top professional musicians in performance one rarely questions their standard of performance skill; they guarantee this. Likewise with Noh.

Having given a brief description of the constituent parts of the Noh play, I shall now describe in more detail the main elements of the performance. I shall begin with the mask.

The Noh Mask: Design and Use

For me, Noh begins and ends with the mask. From the mask, all the character details and performance elements evolve. The mask is the resource centre of the character. Once the mask is designed, then everything else is created to complement that design.

The most interesting discovery I made when examining Noh masks which were used by the Kanze company in Tokyo, is that most of the masks were hundreds of years old.

They bore the marks of age and centuries of use. Scratches, stains, discolouration of the pigments, faded areas where the ties had chaffed the outer layers of paint, all contributed to make subtle changes to the surface psyche of the character. All of these natural ageing processes seem – in the opinion of the senior actors in each school – to enhance the power and serenity of the mask; a mystical mellowing. It is also challenging and stimulating for them to be using a mask which has been worn by generations of actors dating back hundreds of years. It carries its own ghosts with it.

Occasionally, a newly made mask would be worn, its design reproducing to the last hairline scratch, the detail of the original from which it had been copied. It could be safe to assume therefore that, because all new masks are models of their antique originals, as reproductions they have to be inferior, no matter how skilfully they have been carved and painted.

This whole question of reproducing the original forms of the Noh art needs careful scrutiny, and I shall examine it closely in my chapter on the training of the Noh Actor.

At this juncture, I feel quite safe in saying that the skills of the mask maker in Japan are as strong as ever. I make this judgement having spent some time in the workshops of a number of carvers of Noh masks. I shall refer to the work of two whose carving methods are traditionally the same, but whose end results are sometimes very different.

Akiko Taniguchi has been carving Noh masks for over twenty-five years. She was formally trained as a sculptor. All her masks are made for professional performers, and she has a special association with the actors of the Kanze school in Tokyo, making a number of masks for Hideo Kanze, one of its most famous and senior actors.

Each mask takes approximately three months to complete. The time is divided equally between carving and painting. The minimum cost for such a mask will be in the region of £3,000. Apart from making new masks, Ms Taniguchi is an expert mask restorer and has a huge backlog of restoration work which continually interrupts her mask carving.

The wood used is Cypress, being both traditionally acceptable and technically most suitable for carving, having a close-grained, yet lightweight composition.

The mask is completed in three stages. Firstly it is carved to a very fine finish and excessive sanding is unnecessary.

Secondly, the outer surface is prepared with a series of layers of crushed shell bonded with a special glue medium, which are lightly sanded until a perfectly smooth 'egg-shell' surface has developed. Finally layers of pigment and painted features are completed and the 'ageing' process is applied.

It is the way in which the carving and the colouring matches exactly the expression and pallor of the face of the original which attracts the Noh actor to a specific carver's work, for it is the actor alone who makes his decision before each performance as to which mask he will wear to best represent the emotional and physical state of the character he is about to play.

11. Workroom and bench of the mask carver Akiko Taniguchi

Ms Taniguchi is famous for her 'Women' masks. Her studio is a veritable museum of all types of characters in all the categories of women plays. The most enigmatic of these masks, and the most famous is the Ko-Omote mask, the young woman character portrayed by the Shite or Shite-Tsure. Nothing seems 'fixed' in either its outward expression or its inner emotion. Such is the exquisite design of the original that to make a near-perfect copy of this mask is the aim of most Japanese Noh mask-carvers. The features are smooth and seemingly emotionally unlined.

It is this aspect, more than any other, which enables an ambiguity of expression to be discovered when worn by a skilled master of Noh. The more the mask is lined and aged and therefore fixed in a singular expression, the more the wearer is limited in terms of emotional development.

The second mask carver I met was Michishige Udaka. He was of special interest to me because he not only carved masks, but he was also a Shite at the height of his acting career with the Kongo School based in Kyoto the ancient capital of Japan. On a number of occasions he wears his own masks rather than those owned by the school, although he does this only with the ultimate approval of the school's Master.

Whilst Mr Udaka follows the same principles of carving and painting as Ms Taniguchi, he is largely self-taught. He differs in his approach in that he is constantly checking the 'attitudes' of the mask in front of a mirror during its construction. It is extremely rare in my experience that a Shite will spend a lot of time in front of a mirror rehearsing with his masks. As a result of his daily ritual before the mirror and in performance, Mr Udaka has discovered a whole new repertoire of angles and attitudes resulting in a reappraisal of the carving of facial expressions.

It is with a carver and performer of his experience that experiments with new Noh masks will reside, and with whom future generations of mask carvers, playwrights and actors, will reconsider their Noh tradition. He represents a very solitary figure: and whilst he is happily bound as a performer within the training disciplines and repertoire of a professional Noh actor, he will have few opportunities to display his experiments. In any case, such experiments remain outside the continuing world of Noh as practised, and inevitably as he experiences it.

12. Mask carving class given by Michishige Udaka

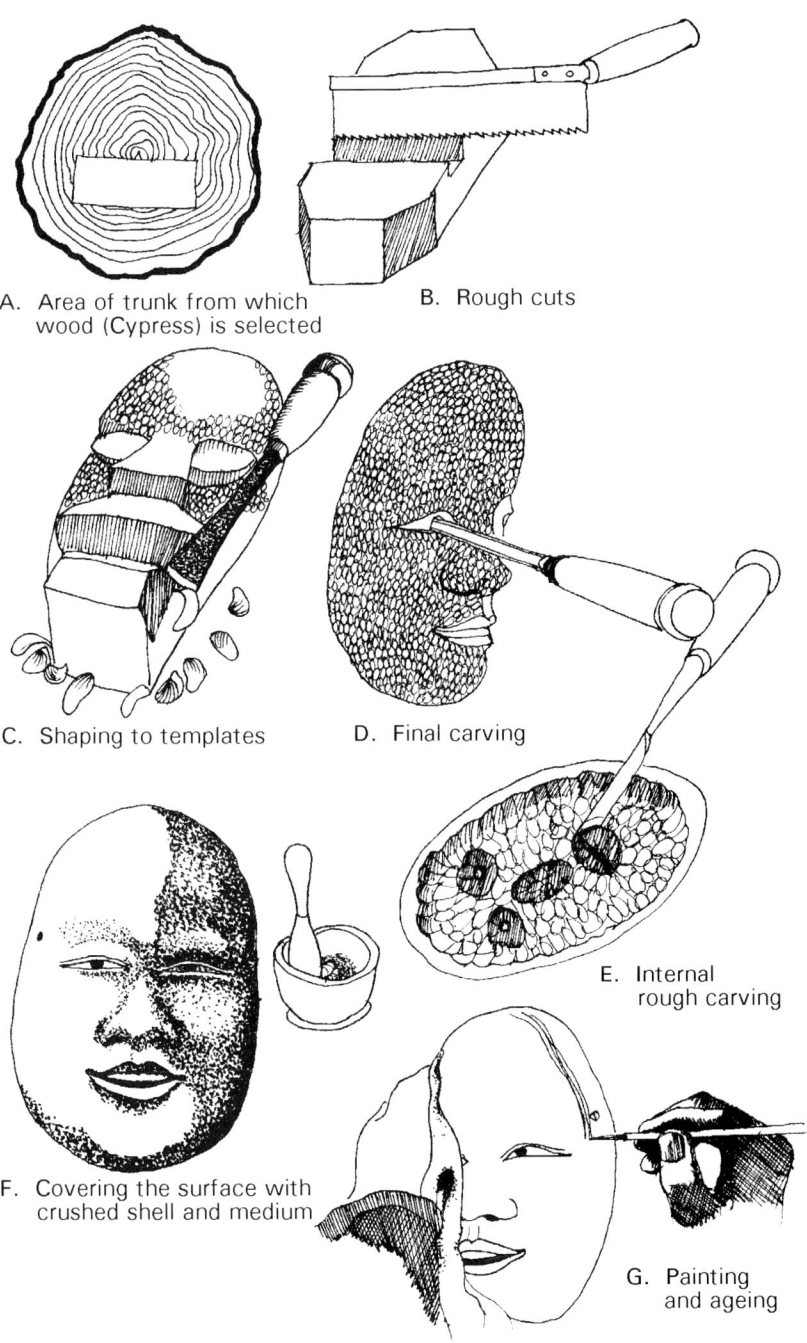

A. Area of trunk from which wood (Cypress) is selected

B. Rough cuts

C. Shaping to templates

D. Final carving

E. Internal rough carving

F. Covering the surface with crushed shell and medium

G. Painting and ageing

13. Making a Noh mask

Properties

These are few in number and are constant in design. The fan is the most commonly used prop and serves as an extension to the motion of the arm, as well as a form of identification in terms of the status of the character using it. It also enhances the emotional detail of the dance and can sometimes represent objects such as a receptacle or drinking vessel.

Props such as a halberd or wand, being close imitations to real objects, locate the character or the environment in which they are used. Thus movement patterns with the halberd which convey familiar actions of conflict, helps to establish a stylised picture of a battle, whilst the wand signals an immediate association with the Shinto ritual of purification.

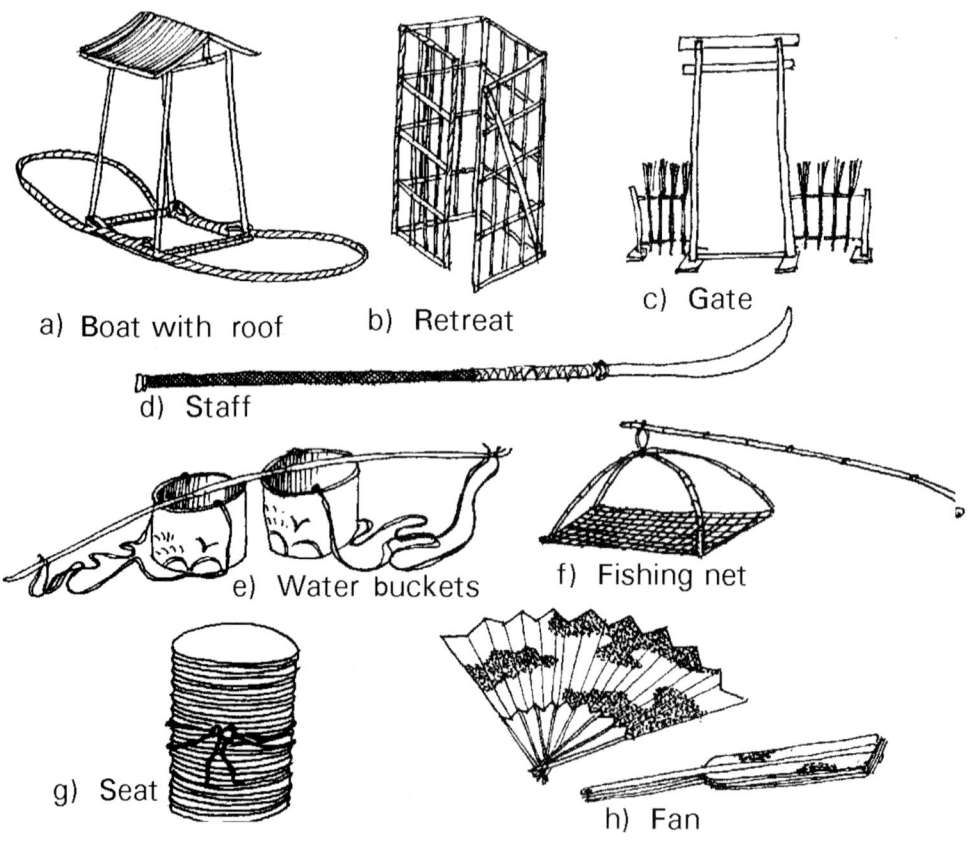

a) Boat with roof b) Retreat c) Gate

d) Staff

e) Water buckets f) Fishing net

g) Seat h) Fan

14. Stage properties

Some props are at the centre of the action of the play such as a drum, shrine, boat or thread-winder. These will either be in the form of a simple bamboo framework suggesting the outline of a boat or carriage in which a number of characters can sit or stand, or they are tiny models which can be used as an emblem – a form of visual aid to illustrate an important part of an anecdote or narrative.

15. Water bucket sequence

Sometimes a framework is draped in a cloth and is used as a screen behind which a Shite may change his costume and mask with the help of the attendants. The cloth is removed and the new character is revealed. Occasionally the same prop can become two or three different things in different locations.

The attendants get the props on and remove them as unobtrusively as possible, as they are discarded. The larger props are set before the scene begins, and removed at its conclusion, and may need more than one attendant to carry them.

Some props are large enough to conceal an actor and are used in this way. Once again it is important to point out that the audience will know that the character is concealed, but it will not lessen the effect of the surprise at the ensuing revelation. It's a bit like waiting for the familiar punch line of a joke and still laughing at its delivery.

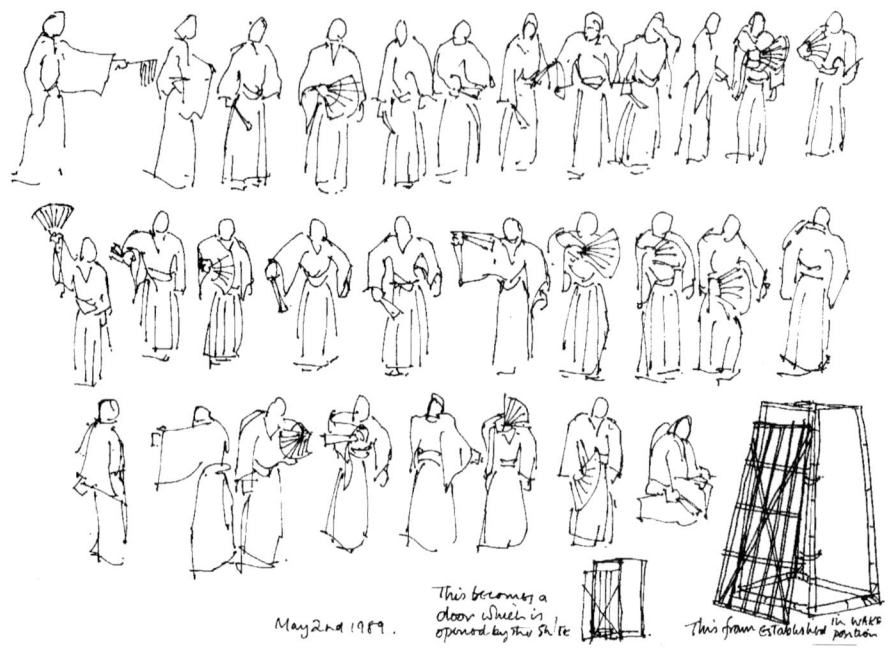

16. Shite sequence

However, props in the Noh play form an intrinsic and expressive part of the meaning and location of time and space. They are as essential to the audience as the text, the music and the dance. They make a simple, clear statement in the midst of the rest of the complexity, as well as helping the actor to conjure some of his most effective moments of theatrical magic.

Many of the props are constructed at the school by the trainee Shite. This is one of their tasks. One cannot imagine a western actor, being involved in any way with the construction of his props, as part of his training. This I think is unfortunate and is one of the reasons why I am especially anxious that actors wearing masks should have a contact with the making of their masks. I shall return to this point later.

Costume

The masked Noh actor, when fully dressed, is almost completely buried in many layers of costume. Only his hands and a small part of his neck and chin are exposed.

The costumes are not simply designed to complement the personality of the character portrayed but are used to identify sex, rank and profession. They also have a historical reference which brings with each design its own link with previous generations; this seems to enhance the intrinsic sense of timelessness. Costumes in Noh add much to the visual effect of the dance.

Colours and shape determine age and mood, as well as personality. Given the limited cut and design of the cloak, kimono and skirt, the actor

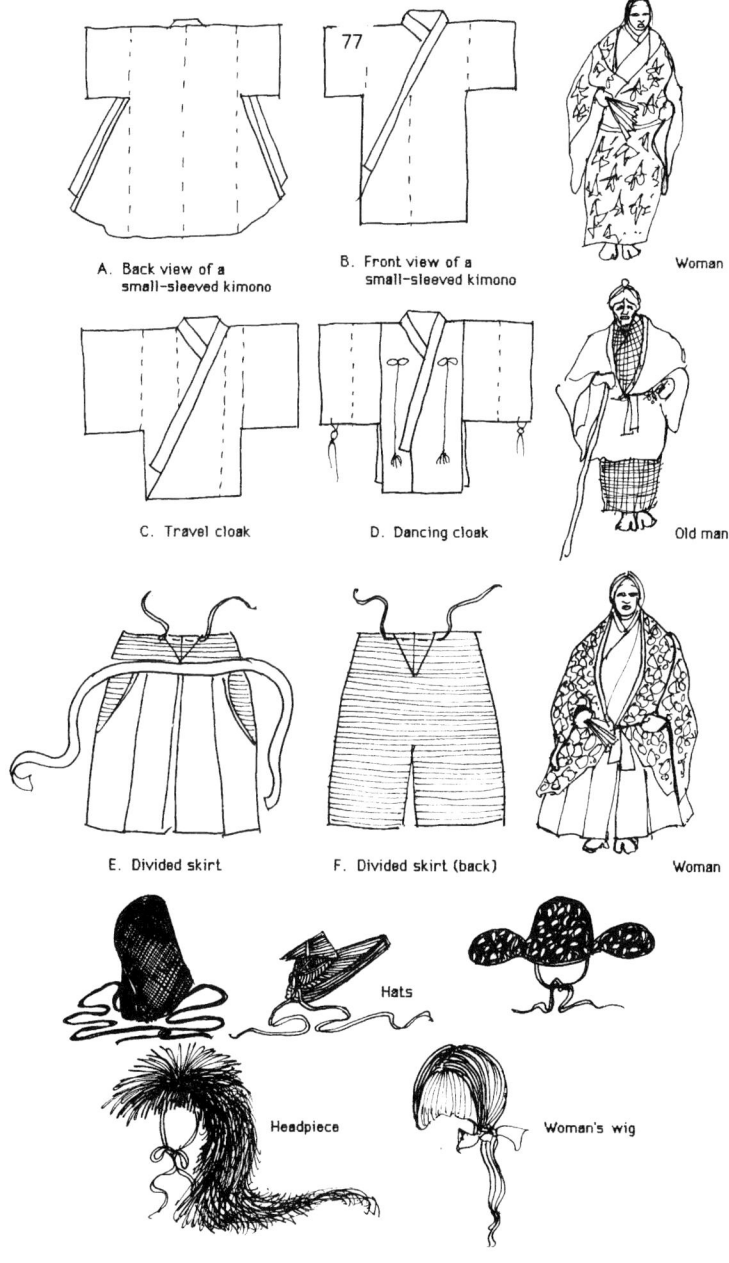

A. Back view of a small-sleeved kimono

B. Front view of a small-sleeved kimono

Woman

C. Travel cloak

D. Dancing cloak

Old man

E. Divided skirt

F. Divided skirt (back)

Woman

Hats

Headpiece

Woman's wig

17. Noh costume, hats and wigs

has to select, from the garments available to him, those combinations which seem to best serve his interpretation of his character within the play at each performance. Rarely will the same combination be repeated, and each variant brings to a performance a sense of novelty.

As mentioned previously, the cut and design of the costume determines a rough framework of what is possible and not possible in terms of the movement in the dance. Thus, steps tend to be small in length, and care has to be taken when the familiar squatting positions are adopted.

The exaggerated kimono sleeves hang, or are twirled, draped, folded, extended, and clasped according to the style and requirements of the dance.

Sometimes this is functional, to keep the sleeves out of the way whilst an important prop is held or clasped; at other times they are used almost like a prop as a vessel for pouring or receiving, or simply as a visual metaphor extending the effect and mood of a particular gesture or pattern of movement.

Given the quality of the silks and brocades used in the making of these exquisite garments, the effect of their use in bringing texture and brilliance to a performance can be breathtaking. They seem to add to the scale and presence of the many spectres being presented. Given, also, the absence of setting and special lighting effects, the focus upon them is total.

Dressing the actor, and caring for the state of his costume during the performance, is an important part of the attendant's work. There is much technical knowledge to be learned such as the folding and draping as well as the application and use of a variety of knots. It takes up to three quarters of an hour for two experienced actors to dress a Shite before a performance.

Over his split-toe socks and his base undergarment, many layers of kimono, cloak and padding will be assembled. Sometimes the actor will be literally stitched into his costume to avoid folds and sleeves from working loose during the performance.

Once the main layers are secure then the appropriate wig is chosen, tied on, combed and styled. This precedes or follows the tying of the mask depending upon the character. For instance a warrior wears his wig over his mask, for a young woman, the mask covers the wig, so the order of the final setting of mask and wig is determined accordingly.

Once again it is important to be reminded that during the performance the attendants will be constantly keeping a keen eye upon the costume of the Shite, in the event of a fold or sleeve shape becoming unsightly when the Shite is squatting or seated and being immediately on hand to rectify it.

Should a skirt become caught against a prop, the appropriate re-alignment will be made – in full view of the audience. This support and care for the protagonists before and during the performance I find so refreshing. The attendants are also actors at different stages of their training and development.

This dressing and attending encourages another aspect of learning. Not only does it show an implicit support for the Shite who is performing, but it allows for an opportunity to work on stage, in front of an audience, without having the pressures of performing a Shite role. An active place to watch, listen and learn, whilst mentally following, in the closest possible proximity, roles which they will eventually include in their own performing repertoire.

Their own contribution will be measured in the unselfish way in which they will remain 'unseen'. This special quality of humility which seems to pervade the Japanese psychology, is one which I shall refer to again and again. Both on and off stage the Noh actors who I met were devoid of egotistical obtrusiveness. I have seen a number of performances where the most experienced and highly regarded Shite or Master of a school, has been an attendant or a member of a chorus.

In Noh there are no stars in the western sense. An audience will appreciate the skills of a top Shite, but will rarely have any knowledge of what the actor looks like or any information about his private lifestyle. The adoration is for the Noh, its stories and characters; the actors who perform it remain largely anonymous servants to it.

Having given a brief description of Noh and its constituent parts, I shall now turn to the most important aspect of this volume.

2

THE TRAINING OF THE NOH ACTOR

Actors in Noh are trained in schools. Each acting character who appears in the Noh cycle is taught in his own specialist school, thus there are separate schools for Shite, Waki and Kyogen. Members of the chorus are usually Shite at various stages of their development, and are therefore trained in the Shite school. There are separate schools also for each of the specialist instrumentalists.

It is perhaps misleading to continue to refer to the training establishments as 'schools' in the western sense, for the Noh actor, especially in the early stages of his training, becomes a devotee to a 'family' of actors, with all that sense of service and devotion to the patriarchal leadership and care which emanates and is reciprocated from its Master.

A 'son' of Noh leads the sort of monastic existence one associates with the priesthood, such is the time and effort he is expected to devote to the learning of his craft.

As he never completes his task, he is always in a state of learning. A pupil of Noh is a pupil for life. It is said that a Noh actor is married to his art and to a large extent this is true; once accepted by his master, he is welcomed into a family. It is to this sense of 'family' with all its 'hand-me-down' learning, inbuilt discipline and secrecy, that I shall refer to, rather than use the term 'school' with all its familiar western connotations.

At the conclusion of this book I shall examine the *Treatises of Zeami* in order to assess how far from the original mould, the present training methods and philosophy of Noh acting has shifted. However, it is worthwhile noting that the original concept of Hana (the development of the Flower) remains untouched. The highest expression of the Noh actor's art is reached when his Hana has blossomed to its most beautiful and richest state, and its display is critically judged as representing the highest possible realisation of physical, vocal, and spiritual technique, hence the highest level of artistry.

There are five main families of Noh, four of which Kanze, Hosho, Kongo and Komparu, have a direct genealogy that has survived the six centuries from the period of Zeami; the fifth, Kita – being the youngest – was formed in the seventeenth century as an offshoot of the Kongo family.

I shall make reference mainly to the methods of training Shite in the Kanze school being the one that I spent most of my time observing whilst in Tokyo and Kyoto.

However, it must be stated, that although the discerning audience will be able to detect small nuances of interpretation of the physical and vocal display of characters in performance, these nuances reflect more the differing personality of each family rather than their training methods and philosophy, which remain fundamentally very similar.

So, what is the basic structural tradition which a Noh actor is expected to follow?

Each family has its inbuilt hierarchy which is based firstly upon 'belonging' by hereditary right, and secondly by age, ability and experience. It is possible for a talented youngster, training in Noh, to be discovered by his teacher (usually a professional Shite) and recommended and then accepted into a Noh family.

Once he has successfully passed through all the various stages of development and been finally accepted into the family, it is possible theoretically for him to receive all the privileges and benefits of 'family' life. Any of his subsequent offspring will enjoy from birth the same opportunities and facilities for becoming a Noh actor as a hereditary Shite should he wish to do so.

The family is headed by its Iemoto, its Master. When he takes on the mantle of head of the family he accepts the responsibility for the continuance of both its artistic standards and its domestic traditions. This is manifested in the way in which the actors are housed and trained, and the way in which their domestic and social lives are supervised and monitored.

This exalted position is handed down from generation to generation, and with it the methods and traditions. It is only comparatively recently, in the twentieth century, that these 'secret' traditions have been released for more public scrutiny. Even now there are rituals and training sessions which are still closely guarded, thus preserving some of the mystique and mystery of 'family'.

Not so the Kanze family. Their doors for me were always open.

The quest to unfold the mysteries of the flower, begins traditionally on the sixth day of the sixth month of the sixth year of a young boy's life; I say 'boy' because there are still very few women training to become Shite in professional Noh – they are part of a tiny but growing minority.

In reality, training can begin almost as soon as the child can walk and talk; he will be exposed to the world of Noh simply by being born into it. The very space in which he lives will include a practice room which duplicates in scale and surface the stage of a Noh theatre. This practice space, in the Noh household will be in constant daily use and will be an unavoidable reference point. Like the 'suitcase' child of a western actor's family, the aura and timetable of the Noh actor's lifestyle will almost inevitably permeate its sensibility, especially if 'it' is a boy.

My first experience of observing the training of a Kokata (boy actor), was in Kyoto at the Kanze household and theatre. The boy was three years old. He had obviously been studying for some time, because he was not only familiar with the role he was studying, but with the basic structure of the dance.

The 'lesson' lasted for about fifteen minutes, and was conducted in the theatre, on the stage. The Shite conducting the lesson was the younger brother of the Iemoto. The lesson began with the traditional, formal, kneeling bow of greeting, the Shite and pupil facing each other a few feet apart.

They began their work centre stage, having arrived through the sliding door upstage left. Whilst the Shite beat out a rhythmical pattern to accompany the choral part mouthed in quiet accompaniment, the pupil established his opening posture with fan, and then, in a strident voice, gave full and rhythmical vent to his chant. When he finished, the Shite led him through a short movement pattern which circumnavigated the down stage area and lead him back to his starting position, having paused and instructed at another position en route.

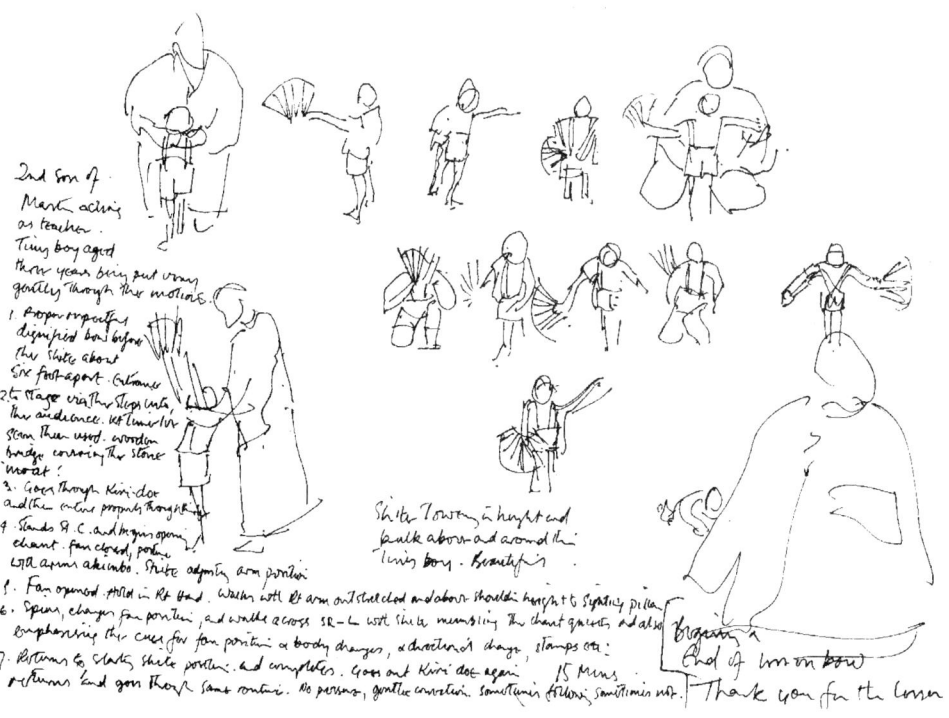

18. Training of a Kokata at the Kanze household, Kyoto

The pupil was 'shown how' by example, in both the way he arranged and moved his body, and delivered his chant.

His limbs were physically adjusted according to the way of the Shite. This had to be done with exacting precision. The Shite showed, the pupil copied. This short sequence was repeated three or four times, and then

19(a). Rehearsal sequence I of a Kokata

19(b). Rehearsal sequence II of a Kokata

19(c). Rehearsal sequence III of a Kokata

the lesson came to its conclusion with a similar kneeling (seiza) and bowing 'thank you' ritual to that which began it.

The whole lesson had taken approximately fifteen minutes, and had been conducted in a formal, yet caring and gentle manner. At no time did the pupil display any sense of anxiety, nor was he patronised, and he returned smilingly happy to his waiting mother.

The atmosphere surrounding the lesson contained its own conditions of self-discipline. There was however a sense of fun in learning and achieving. There was nothing unusual in this; I have observed many instrumental and dance teachers in the west employing this method in a similar atmosphere and with similar results. But I have never witnessed anything resembling this in drama or theatre. The picture of this forty-year old Shite, at the height of his performing career, gently and carefully guiding this tiny three year old through the first stages of Noh, will forever remain locked in my memory.

'Showing how' and copying what has been shown, is the method of Noh. Thus, lessons in all the separate elements of Noh, are conducted in this manner. This is the way in which all the Noh families believe their skills and traditions will continue to be preserved for future generations to experience.

There is never a sense in which this method of teaching and thus the form of Noh becomes so fossilised that it begins to decay. There is a language, form and meaning which has remained constant throughout its history. Only when the form and meaning of Noh becomes so unrecognisable from the inner and external nature of the society which surrounds it, and to which it relates, will it develop a new language.

And yet the essence of its survival remains in its novelty; the way in which each performance or 'rehearsal' re-presents its original with a unique energy and freshness, and makes the kind of direct contact with its audience in such a way as to continue to embrace and enrich it.

I wish to digress a moment and consider the more familiar training of a cabinet maker. Firstly he must learn about the special qualities of wood, its growth, the differing properties of each species, whether it can bend happily, undertake the stress of weight and pressure, be cut and jointed more effectively in construction than be carved. He must learn how to construct with it, the path of learning taking him into the tool box and onto the bench. He must learn how to hone and use tools to shape and fashion lengths of wood, cut joints, and so on and so on.

The list of skills needed to be learned is endless. He learns by imitating what he is taught by a craftsman who is passing on the basics of what he has learned. Although the end product, the acquisition of skills, is the same, the method of showing and learning will vary according to the personality.

But only when he has learned those skills, and can work without thinking of them – because he can recall them and re-energise them as he needs them – can he design and build his furniture, embodying the spirit of the materials and his craft using time-proven methods, and also demonstrate his uniqueness of spirit.

I suppose the work of the Thompson Brothers of North Yorkshire is a case in point, where their craft of making furniture in oak has continued for generations and is in greater demand than ever. The wood is prepared in the way of its founder George, and the adze is still swung to produce the familiar finish of the table tops. The joints are dowelled and the famous mouse adorns the legs and edges of tables and chairs.

But this furniture is considered original and not reproduction, and is admired and bought as such. Such traditions and skills are thought of as being delightful to purchase, preserve and invest in. They bring both a practical and an aesthetic sensibility to a household.

Similarly with the Noh. The *Kokata* (Child actor) must learn how to sit, to stand, to travel, to dance and to chant. The standard of all of these skills is directly related to the roles in the repertoire which are created for him. It is as though the parts have been designed with the development of the *Kokata* in mind.

The degree of involvement and the skills required by the *Kokata* depend upon the play chosen. Many plays include them in their cast and so there is another very practical reason why the Noh actor begins his training so early.

The emphasis in the training at this stage is on 'doing'. There is no book opened, no 'score' referred to. The child simply settles opposite his teacher and repeats the chant or movement he is taught.

On many occasions the teacher will 'mark' the patterns of movement and spend much time re-adjusting the position of feet, legs, trunk, arms, hands, head, and fan, guiding the child through these movements until the basics have been grasped. The teacher is then able to stand away, scrutinise and correct the child's dance from a distance.

As soon as the child is considered ready for exposure to an audience, he will be cast in a walk-on *Kokata* role perhaps with several others, where all that will be required of him is to enter, sit for a short time and then exit. All this is possible within the context of a Noh play such as 'Kurama Tengu' in which several *Kokata* appear on a flower-viewing outing.

This brief performance experience introduces the *Kokata* not only to the discipline of presenting his newly acquired skills to a sympathetic audience, but also to all the many preparatory dressing rituals backstage.

When the *Kokata* is not preparing for a specific performance he is taught *Shimai* which are short dance sections appropriated from traditional plays, performed with complementary chorus. In any case, the child does not receive formal voice lessons, nor will he ever do so. This follows the tradition of the actors of the Peking Opera where the 'voice' is developed as a result of its use in rehearsal and performance. It is developed simply by using it.

In Noh, the weight for the dance and the voice is firmly located in the lower abdomen. The actor 'sits' on this energy resource and uses it to 'centre' his voice and performance. This is how the unseen tension in Noh is created.

This base is formed by the weight of the body being shifted slightly forward, so that the control of travelling is automatically corrected through the balls of the feet.

The upper trunk is straight and thrusting, the lower part of the spine being pulled in. The arms, extended between the shoulders and the waist, are slightly curved with the elbows out, and the hands are in front of the trunk.

The basic body position of the Noh actor is called *Kamae*, and its location is earthbound rather than elevated. It seems to make a logical association with the natural laws of gravity.

This is the basic posture of Noh. It is very strong and energy-charged. From this base all movement develops and returns. When the posture has been learned, it looks totally natural and relevant to the dance patterns of Noh. Even with very strong and fast spins and turns, the performance remains centred around this basic posture, and mastery of it is the lifetime preoccupation of the Noh actor.

20. Basic posture of the Noh actor

Once the movements begin, then the *Suriashi*, the 'sliding feet' walk is employed. It is this walk in particular which seems to especially identify the movement of the Noh actor.

Suriashi is the art of sliding the foot, ensuring that it never completely leaves the floor, even when the toes are lifted slightly at the end of a step.

The stillness and control of the *Suriashi* depends not only upon the strength and control of the *Kamae* (basic body position), but also in the control of the slightly bent knees which act as shock absorbers to maintain a level and erect gliding movement. And whilst the limbs will be hidden by layers of costume, there must be no sense of awkwardness or tension in movement. The gliding must appear natural and effortless, the technique invisible.

Finally, the movement forms are called *Kata* (pattern), and whilst one or two of the *Kata* are designed for specific plays, the majority are used in all plays. The same basic movements allow a contextual novelty of expression without altering the structure of the movement. This hints of the versatility of the Noh form. It is extraordinary how a familiar pattern of movement can take on a completely separate identity depending upon the skill of the performer and the nature of the play.

These three elements, all 'patch' together to form the basic shape and energy resource of the Noh actor in performance. The *Kamae* is the base from which the *Suriashi* and the *Kata* are generated. Any imbalance in these and the aesthetic effect will be instantly diluted.

These three elements are the beginning, and the constant returning point of the physical training of the Noh actor. They remain, throughout his life, his continuous reference. He cannot practice them enough. It is like the scales for the musician and the bar work for the dancer; by necessity they form an essential part of a daily ritual.

While these physical elements are being taught, the intrinsic rhythmical patterns are being mentally lodged, both through the *Utai* (the chant) and the *Kata*. Again, the language of the drumming and the pulse of the chorus is not taught with any formality at this stage. Its presence is inherent in the 'showing' of the *Utai*, although all the Utai that is taught is only what is needed by the *Kokata* in performance.

During this initial period the *Kokata* will follow a normal programme of primary education within the state system. In fact it is becoming increasingly the norm for trainee Shite to follow a continuous course of academic training up to and including University level, before making the final and total commitment to the Noh way of life; the training at the later stages fitting around the University timetable.

The pressures endured by a trainee Shite at this time, in terms of his having to combine a commitment to both his academic and Noh development, is extreme, with little or no time for recreation.

From his initial introduction to the formality of Noh training, the *Kokata* will increase the number of times each week he spends with his Shite teacher, and he will learn a variety of *Kokata* roles which will become more challenging as time and ability progress.

There will be no formal testing by practical or oral examination in order to measure his developing skills, and his ability to perform, but there will be a close watch on the sense of natural *Yugen* which is displayed. This 'spirit' or 'grace' is what is deemed important.

The nearest parallel to *Yugen* in western terms, is a stage 'presence'; something about the performer which sets them apart in the acting space and is compelling to watch, even if they are still. It is not until the next stage, when the boy is undergoing physical and emotional changes, that a closer and more rigid programme of training and scrutiny is observed.

This second development from say eleven or twelve up to the age of twenty or older, is called the *Uchideshi* stage. *Uchideshi* means 'house disciple'; and it is during this stage, that traditionally, the trainee Shite will be resident in the household of his teacher and master.

Depending upon the size and the scale of the administration of his family, the *Uchideshi* will be schooled only by the Iemoto (Master) or one of his immediate family. Not only will he be subjected to a rigorous training programme but he will also have to spend some of his time doing domestic chores; not unlike the odd-jobbing expected by the initiate assistant stage-manager in western theatres.

He will be subjected to the labours of his status and age within the system, doing much fetching and carrying for those actors in seniority above him. This state changes as his status develops. The *Uchideshi* in turn is looked after by the household; his training and living expenses being taken care of.

His acceptance into the household therefore is a major step forward. If he is literally 'one of the family' being the son or nephew of a Shite or the Master's family, then his entry is almost automatic. His acceptance will be scrutinised with greater care if he is not 'family' and has emerged through the alternative route of the amateur system. This will depend firstly upon his ability, and secondly upon the strength of the outside financial support available. Once accepted, it is unlikely that he will deviate from his chosen path. There is an unconditional acceptance of this contract with his family and his Noh schooling for life.

Training is daily, seven days a week, and sometimes during holidays. Whilst the *Uchideshi* will continue to refer to his teacher for instruction on a one to one basis, his will also become subjected to a group teaching practice which will be both formal and informal.

He will spend much time sharing the practice space and time with his *Uchideshi* colleagues, taking turns with them to dance Shite roles and to observe and chant in chorus. His practice times will, at this stage, still fit around his formal secondary education timetable, but the demands of his Noh training will determine at what time he begins and ends each day's practice.

Some of his practice sessions will be observed by his teacher and will be subject to criticism and correction. During the other 'shared' sessions, he will learn simply from his observance of others, most of whom will be much more experienced than him.

This is one of the most important aspects of the Noh actor's continued training. He is always being taught by watching and doing. There is always something new that emerges during practice, rehearsal, and

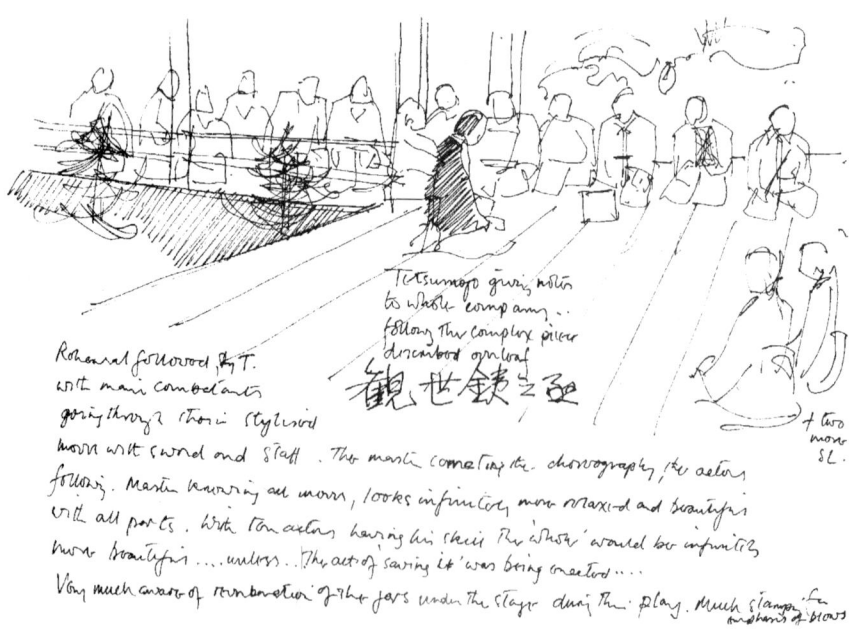

21. Iemoto Tetsumojo giving notes at a rehearsal

performance for the Shite to consider and there is *the proper time to absorb and learn.*

He will in fact spend more of his performance time in a state of participation in chorus or attendance than he will in the protagonist role of Shite, and his whole training philosophy encourages him to always take note of what he sees and senses from the performance of others: a very important, practical expression of humility.

One or two important developments will have taken place during this period. The *Uchideshi's* voice will be settling into its adult cadence. If it settles quickly then there will probably be no break in his opportunity to perform, whereas if the voice is unstable for any length of time, he will have to wait until it has settled before being exposed to public scrutiny once more.

But during this early stage, another difference in the one-to-one sessions with his teacher will have taken place. He will now be extending his repertoire of plays and Shite roles by 'reading' them from the official, family '*Utaibon*', a sort of vocal score which includes the markings of the rhythm of drumming, and also tiny drawings indicating the physical changes in posture at crucial moments of the dance.

So, having studied this new, and quite complex written exposition of each play, he will be able to learn by himself the chants and the 'dialogue' of the Shite, and bring this learning to his teacher, who will then check and criticise what has been absorbed, adopting the familiar, imitative teaching method.

There is a special moment which all Shite remember. It will be unheralded, unexpected, and there will be no spoken reference to the change in status during or after. It occurs when their teacher asks them to show and chant without his having demonstrated first. It is a private and special moment. The pupil knows that he has passed through an important stage in his development. It is a recognition and acknowledgment that a solid base of oral and physical skills have been absorbed and fixed.

A *Uchideshi* spends as much time learning the backstage skills as he does the acting skills. There is no formal teaching which shows him how to take care of the folding and packing and maintenance of costumes; of the making of props and how to transport them to and from their location on stage; of how to costume an actor, for no actor costumes himself. He must assimilate these skills through observation, with the help of more experienced *Uchideshi* and then practice in his own time.

There is also the question of etiquette; the need to quickly recognise the backstage and performance preparation rituals, as well as the correct conduct towards other performers. Some of these rituals are commonplace in Japanese society and will be already known and practised, but many are peculiar to Noh. They form another important ingredient in the complex and unique atmosphere, which contributes so much to the mental preparation and performance focus, for the ensemble of actors.

It is during this stage that the *Uchideshi* will learn to wear the mask. He will have handled the masks before, removing them and repacking them with consummate care into their silk bags and carrying boxes. But he will not have the opportunity to wear them until he plays his first Shite role.

It is this stage that is of particular interest to me, for the use of the mask in Noh is central to my philosophy. I wanted to discover exactly how a Noh actor learns to use his mask and the methods which he adopts to develop his skill.

It was difficult to find actors willing to expound upon the use of mask in Noh. After many frustrated attempts to breach the hallowed grounds of backstage preparation, I eventually had the opportunity to spend some time with three Shite.

Two were the Masters of their respective Kanze schools in Tokyo and Kyoto, and were at the height of their performing careers, whilst the third was a young Shite of the Kita school who should eventually inherit the exalted Iemoto (Master) status.

Their views on mask were identical. Firstly that the stylised physical language of the Noh dance developed and became 'fixed' because of the mask, and secondly that it is the spirit of the mask which has pervaded and nourished a consistency of performance reference handed down from generation to generation.

This, along with the costume, has helped to sustain continuity of style and effect in performance; the preservation of the spirit and of the standards of performance during the Renaissance. The fact that the same masks are still used, tends to support the belief that each mask carries for its wearer the generations of Shite who have presented that character in performance.

In the ageing process of the mask, each generation has an increasingly widening reference to the ghostly spirits of the past, and thus has the potential to extend a more profound psychological study of the character, than the preceding one.

The most interesting aspect of the mask training is that to some extent, many of the physical attitudes which are used by the Noh actor in performance are already set in the shape of the dance. Most actors rehearse without mask. They will only wear the mask as they get very close to a performance date, and even then this is not guaranteed as they wish to make a final embodied contact with the spirit of the character at the very last moment before presenting that character on stage.

It is worth noting at this point, that there is a direct parallel with this detail of preparation with the mask for performance as the Egungun of the Masquerade of Nigeria, described in Volume 4 of this series.

All the time they are learning the dance, they are shaping and articulating the physical language of their character by placing and moving their heads as though they are wearing the mask. The only time that they use the mirror is at the moment before they are about to go on stage. The time in the mirror room is hallowed. After the dressing, the mask is carefully scrutinised so that the actor can externalise his character, and pull himself within it by the act of putting on and absorbing the inherited spirit of the mask.

Apart from the Shite Michishige Udaka whom I mentioned earlier, this was the practice followed by all the Noh Shite I observed. It is this aspect of the Noh training which makes me uneasy when I consider the way in which the traditions are preserved, using the 'hand-me-down' apprenticeship method. Like Michishige Udaka, I feel the Noh actor's prime reference in terms of the character and the play has to be the mask.

He cannot spend enough time wearing it as he trains and rehearses. The pre-performance Mirror Room exercise should be the most important part of the daily ritual. Like the dancer at the bar in front of the mirror, it is always there and is only removed during the performance, the audience – in effect – becoming the mirror. The performance therefore becomes conceived objectively by the actor. He must externalise the

22. Performance: *Tama-Kazura*, Hosho Theatre, Tokyo

43

character's inner psyche and be in total control of the technical elements which convey this to the audience.

Not that it is often possible technically to refer to self in the mirror when wearing a mask simply because of the focus that is determined by the position of the mask on the face and the size and shape of the eye or sight holes.

Some of the Noh masks are traditionally smaller than the average sized face, and so the actor must compensate accordingly, sometimes having to resort to looking through the nostrils of the mask in extreme cases.

In order to set the mask on the face so that all the idiosyncrasies of mask design and the human features can be accommodated happily, small pads are strategically placed between the inside of the mask and the features of the actor to ensure stability and comfort.

There must always be someone 'outside' the mask, to help the actor discover the ways in which the mask can be animated, in order to bring the character to life. This is usually the Iemoto or one of the senior Uchideshi. The actor then has to be able to recall the angles and shapes of the dance with such precision, if he is to be able to repeat with exactitude, the emotional details he has demonstrated in practice. Whatever happens, both in practice and in performance, the spirit of the mask and the performer must complement each other totally.

There is another important element to which the *Uchideshi* is introduced at this stage, and that is a fixed programme of training in the other specialties of Noh.

He is expected to reach a high standard of skill in drumming and in the flute, although he will not be expected to perform in either. It is imperative that he reaches this level of skill and understanding so that he is totally aware of the rhythmical and notational structures of all the other elements of the Noh performance, matching that of his own as Shite. He will be taught these skills either alone, or with a small group of actors who are at a similar stage of their training.

The *Uchideshi* stage may last from say five to fifteen years, and depends upon many circumstances, such as age, when training began, personal, financial, educational and domestic considerations, and the rate of progress during training.

In the mid-twenties, the *Uchideshi* stage gives way to the penultimate stage of *Jun-Shokobun* or 'pre-full professional'. Their status of independence increases. They take on more difficult roles, and their reference to the Master of the school for permission to take on work outside the school – such as teaching – is no longer needed. However, he will be expected to continue with his lessons with the Master and it is essential at this stage for him not to lose proper contact with this vital training resource.

It is during this stage also that the more exacting roles are considered and the challenges met. Permission to perform these is still in the hands of the Master. As a result of seeing his pupil perform these roles a Master will determine whether or not to grant the 'full-professional' status of *Shokabun* which will establish his graduation finally into the adult world of the professional Noh actor. Although the requirements to achieve this status differ from school to school, the ultimate decision rests with each Master.

Thus the 'team' of adult actors in any family, and their standard of performing skills as individuals and as a chorus, depends almost totally upon the head of each family, and their reputation as a school will be measured accordingly.

Progress for the Noh actor from this point is determined totally by the new plays he will be exposed to and expected to learn. Each new play will have its own special skill elements to acquire and master.

Some of the early plays a Shite performs require a considerable facility for physical agility, having a number of energetic and almost gymnastic dance sequences, which contain exchanges of combat with staff, sword, or wand.

The most exacting roles for the Shite at the height of his acting power, demand long sequences of subtle, slow patterns of movement and stillness.

Long sequence of very physical
threatening moves directed at young shogun.

23. Rehearsal, Tessen-Kai

24. Performance: *Yoroboshi*, Hosho Theatre, Tokyo

25. Performance: *Kokaji*, National Noh Theatre, Tokyo

These need considerable physical control and mental strength: long sequences of very slow dance patterns which sustain an undisturbed heightened state of grace (yugen). They would be impossible to perform to any recognisable level of Noh if the years of training which had preceded them, had not been totally and meticulously prepared.

As with all theatre forms, the survival and financing of Noh depends very much upon its patronage, whether by the state, private individual or both. It is fair to say that without the support of the enthusiastic amateur performer, professional Noh Theatre in Japan would struggle to maintain its present standards, both artistic and financial.

Once Noh actors reach the Uchideshi stage in their training, they are able to begin the fairly lucrative business of teaching Utai and Shimai to their amateur devotees – with the permission of their Iemoto. The teaching is tested in performance conditions, by presenting of recital versions of suitable sections from Noh plays. All those invited to take part in these recitals (usually all the pupils of the Shite) will pay large sums of money for the privilege. Other professional Noh actors will also be invited (and paid for) to make up the chorus and add their experience to the proceedings.

Once again, this system of remuneration for the professional Noh actor is not dis-similar to the private teaching offered by musicians and dancers in the West to supplement their income.

There are many obvious, added advantages for the professional Noh actor who teaches. Apart from breaking down the technique he has learned over many years, and constantly re-evaluating what he knows through the process of teaching, he will view many of these classes as personal training sessions.

It is also highly likely that his pupils will attend the performance of his Noh school. It is they in particular who can be seen paying very close attention to the chant score throughout the performances.

Amateurs usually begin their Noh training when they are adults, which is one of the main reasons why they cannot hope to attain the high level of performance skills of the professional, who, like the musician has begun his training at a very early age. They attend with the same enthusiasm as those in our western Adult Education Institutes or sports clubs, and are taken up with the same recreational outlook.

I briefly mention this world of the Noh amateur only to indicate the important financial and artistic support they give to their professional counterparts. At this time, there is more support for the continuation and growth of Noh than at any other time in its long history.

Given Japan's preoccupation with sustaining a strong economy and its premier position in the world's money market, it is refreshing to note that financial support for this traditional art form is still deemed a considerable worthy investment by private and public bodies.

26. Performance: *On Funa-Benkai*, National Noh Theatre, Tokyo

But to return to the training of the Noh actor. The celebration of his maturity as a performer is his invitation to perform a ritual dance called *Okina*. Of 'Okina' Takabayashi Koji, an actor of the Kita School, had this to say:

> 'Okina is the source of all Noh. In Okina lies the spiritual core of Noh and from Okina stems many of the technical bases. Once I wear the mask, I am in communion with the god inside me, with the universal part that transcends the mundane. The whole body, not just the mask, expresses the emotions read as being in the mask.
>
> 'The life force that reaches upward and outward, that works to encompass all, no matter how sad the story, no matter how fearsome the vision, is at its core a celebration (shugen). Performing, I am completed through communion and I hope the audience senses the celebration and goes away purified too.'

This seems a good point to leave the training of the Noh actor as I observed it and consider the thoughts and teachings of the founder of the form and its philosophy, Zeami.

3

AN EVALUATION OF THE TREATISES OF ZEAMI

Ours must be considered an art of pleasure. It should therefore render the hearts of its spectators gentle and mild.[1]

It is my view that all actors should read *The Major Treatises of Zeami* and act upon it. 'On The Art of Noh Drama' is almost unheard of in the west and yet it is the most complete extant selection of authentic writings on a philosophy of acting and actor-training, which has survived since it became established in the fourteenth century, and more importantly, has sustained its influence upon each succeeding generation of Japanese Noh actors almost without question or alteration.

It is very relevant that Zeami should have expressed similar concerns about the state of the art of theatre in his era.

*'I deeply regret the fact that our art already
seems in a state of decline'.*[2]

It is with this 'state' in mind, as well as the need to fix a secret document of Noh philosophy for succeeding generations of Noh actors, that he wrote...

'I do not intend that the various things I have written in The Teachings on Style and the Flower should be shown to the world, but rather that they might serve as a legacy for my descendants'.[3]

It is not my intent to reveal the detailed 'secrets' of the Treatises; they stand by themselves as rich resources to be devoured for instruction and inspiration. Rather I shall make some general observations on the writings of Zeami by way of introduction, to enable the reader to catch a sense of the 'spiritual' almost mystical, hypnotic atmosphere which surrounds the Noh performer and his performance. In any case, the Treatises do not reveal the details of the day-by-day programme of exercises designed to develop graduated stages of co-ordination and physical agility.

These are the preserve of the Iemotos (Masters) of each school who are in 'possession' of the methodology and pass this on first-hand to their

---

[1] Zeami, F. M. *On the Art of Noh Drama, The Major Treatises* (Translated by J. Thomas Rimer and Yamazaki Masakazu. Princeton University Press, 1984) p. 247.
[2] Zeami, F. M. p. 37.   [3] Zeami, F. M. p. 37.

49

pupils; part of the continuing element of secrecy which surrounds and 'protects' the continuance of Noh. I shall describe in some detail the general programme of training for Noh actors, currently being implemented at the Kanze school, later in this chapter.

At this point it is worth recalling from the first book in this series the important common links which I discovered exist between the 'legacy' of Noh left to us by Zeami and with the theatre experiments and philosophies of Meyerhold, Stanislavski, Grotowski and Brook.

Zeami completed the first of the treatises *Teachings on Style And The Flower* in 1402 when he was forty, and completed the eighth *Learning The Way* in 1430 when he was sixty-eight.

In the same year that his son Motoyoshi transcribed the *Reflections on Art*, Zeami also wrote a number of other treatises on the music and chant in Noh, and an account of his experiences whilst exiled on the island of Sado at the end of his life. He died in 1443.

Zeami inherited his role as second master of the Kanze when he was only nineteen. By the time he came to commence his writing of the Treatises he had written and composed an enormous output of new and successful Noh plays, and had performed the main Shite parts in most of them. He was at the height of his profession and so was able to write from his considerable experience. All that he wrote, he had learned, taught, and implemented to consolidate the new Noh philosophy.

It was as a result of his theatrical experiments and developments, and those of his father, that the Noh genre was to become established and lasting. When reading the treatises, the actor/playwright/teacher/director's voices proclaim their passionate, living reference. Zeami's resonance bursts from one who has experienced and learned all that he demands from others.

There is an over-riding tone of humility and grace which permeates the whole Noh philosophy. Paradoxically, in the West, the 'star' system tends to promote the reverse, a kind of self-propagating, brash conceit which is linked with media exposure and financial remuneration. In the West it is usually the actor's face and personality which seems to dominate each role he is asked to play. The 'lead' actor rather than the main character is what tends to be paid for and displayed.

In Noh, each element of music, dance and chorus, is subservient to the other; there is a competitive will to work for domination without actually achieving it. In Noh there is much listening and observing, much invisible cuing and watching. The main actors are heavily constumed and concealed behind a full mask.

In the posters, which advertise the Noh, it is the main character which is displayed disguising completely the actor who is playing the role. I mention this only to offer an appropriate precursor to the main concept of the Noh philosophy, and hence the training which supports it – that of the symbol of the flower.

> *'The Flower symbolises the principle that lies at the deepest recesses of our art. To know the meaning of the Flower is the most important element in understanding the Noh, and its greatest secrets. Only the character of an actor formed by such a thorough training can know the seed of the Flower, for before he can know the Flower, he must know the seed. The Flower blooms from the imagination; the seed represents merely the various skills of our art.'* [4]

The ultimate:

> *'Thus an actor who has mastered every aspect of his art can be said to hold within him the seeds of flowers that bloom in all seasons, from the plum blossoms of early spring, to the chrysanthemums of the fall. As he possesses all the Flowers, he can perform in response to any expectations on any occasion.'* [5]

Zeami has much to say about novelty. Here I think lies the heart of the main purpose behind all the training and preparation to which the Noh actor submits himself. It is a freshness, excitement and energy associated with a 'first performance' to which an actor addresses the skills he has acquired so that there is that sense of expectancy and wonder at the novelty and uniqueness of each performance.

> *'The Flower represents a mastery of technique and thorough practice, achieved in order to create a feeling of novelty.'* [6]

> *'The flower of the actor is possible, precisely because the audience does not know where that flower may be located.'* [7]

> *'An actor should plan to repeat himself only once in a three to five year period so as to create a sense of novelty for his audience.'* [8]

The development of a Noh actor, both in his preparation and in performance, is compared to the propagation, growth and blossoming of a flower in all its uniqueness and its many guises. There is the 'temporary bloom' of the natural appearance and beauty of a young boy, fresh to the Noh, who eventually, during adolescence, 'loses his first flower' when his voice breaks and 'his movements become awkward'. [9]

There is the next stage when a performer has acquired many of the Noh skills in movement and voice, and who begins to attract attention from the public because his 'Flower is a new and fresh one'. With it goes the accompanying warning, that should an actor believe that he is as

---

[4] Zeami, F. M. pp. 29–30.   [5] Zeami, F. M. p. 53.   [6] Zeami, F. M. p. 53.
[7] Zeami, F. M. p. 59.   [8] Zeami, F. M. p. 56.   [9] Zeami, F. M. p. 5.

praiseworthy in his performing as the public regard him, then:

> 'Such an attitude is an enemy to the actor. For such is not the true
> Flower ... it would indeed be a shame if this early Flower, which actually
> represents only the the actor's first level of accomplishment, should some-
> how be fixed in the actor's thoughts, so that he sees this phase as the cul-
> mination of his art, and therefore indulges himself in what is a deviation
> from the true path ... One who believes that this temporary Flower is the
> real Flower is one who has separated himself from the true way. Such is the
> situation of the young actor ... that if he thinks he has attained a higher level
> of skill than he has reached, however, he will lose even the level that he has
> achieved.'[10]

The mid-thirties is the crucial time when the actor 'will have mastered his art to a level that will permit no decline.'[11]

'Even in the case of superior a actor, if he is filled with pride over his mastery of the Noh, his art will dwindle.'[12] There is no room whatsoever for an actor to short-cut any stages of evolution of the Noh craft or character. Any hint of pride or arrogance, will stifle growth and mar fulfilment.

However, once he has found the ultimate beauty of the Flower, then he will inevitably, begin the slow decline in physical beauty but still retain the Flower. 'The art of Noh, even if the foliage is slight and the tree grows old, still retains its blooms.'[13]

But the true Flower is displayed in all its novelty and grace, and it is this sense of freshness in performance which must be the aim of all actors; the ability to surprise and amaze. 'The Flower represents the very life of our art.'[14]

Zeami demands from his disciples that true humility of learning from others and of sharing of skills, recognising shortcomings in self, and constantly re-evaluating. No actor can ignore the performance of others irrespective of their ability.

No matter how unskilled an actor may be, if there is an attractive quality in his performance, superior players should study what he has done.

This is the best means to further self-improvement ... 'the skilful actor must serve as a model for the unskilled actor: and the unskilled player must serve as a model for the skilled player. Such is the very principle on which to proceed.'[15]

There is a chronological development and expectancy. Each stage seems to be measured approximately in decades. Beginning at six and concluding at fifty, Zeami goes through each decade with a concise

---

[10] Zeami, F. M. pp. 6–7. [11] Zeami, F. M. p. 115. [12] Zeami, F. M. p. 25.
[13] Zeami, F. M. p. 9. [14] Zeami, F. M. p. 23. [15] Zeami, F. M. p. 25.

description of what should be achieved at each stage, accompanied by the appropriate warning that at no point can the actor afford to rest upon his laurels.

Once the body and the voice have settled with practice and maturity, and the multiplicity of skills particular to Noh properly absorbed, only then can the individual art of each actor develop and progress to the peak of perfection. Crucially, the constant reference and return to the basic skills learned at an early stage by the Noh actor in training, is another element which reminds me of the training of Dancers and Musicians in the West.

Zeami refers to the 'high degree of refinement' to which all actors aspire but which is only achieved after many years of work. Zeami always refers to the actor's work; the amount of continuous effort needed to learn and perfect the necessary skills to perform Noh with any degree of beauty and grace. The treatises are peppered with such quotes as..'practiced assiduously,' and 'hard work and practice.'

He describes the 'Level' at which the actor eventually reveals his inborn talents and its state, as being one of 'Magnitude'. If either of these of conditions is the aspiration of the actor, then his present 'level' of artistic skill will decline, for such things as level and Magnitude cannot be sought after, they reveal themselves only after a great deal of very hard training, conducted in an atmosphere devoid of arrogance and selfishness.

> 'After arduous practice, and when all the dust of artistic ostentatiousness has been washed off an actor, he may suddenly find that Magnitude arrives of itself, as it were.'[16]

When Zeami talks of the real mastery of Noh he is talking about the display of skills which seem to effortlessly blend together into one sublime whole all the performance elements which inhabit the stage.

A genuine union of music and movement represents a command by the actor of the most profound principles of the art of Noh. When he speaks of real mastery, it is to this principle that he refers ...

> 'the artist who can truly fuse them into one shows the greatest, highest talent of all... he will have learned how to give a strong performance and how to give that performance the quality of Grace as well. He will truly be a masterful performer.'[17]

Zeami has much to say about the audience; the need to listen to its character, feel its contribution, and embrace it. He refers to the many different types of audience and the type of performance they can truly appreciate.

---

[16] Zeami, F. M. p. 26.   [17] Zeami, F. M. pp. 27–28.

'As far as audiences are concerned, they will only give their undivided attention to the most gifted players.'[18]

Similarly he is concerned with the actor's awareness of when and how to deliver a chant or a significant movement. He is very careful to lay out in detail the pitfalls and the joy of an actor's need to know exactly how to 'Match the Feeling of the Moment'. His senses should be alive to the numerous points of expectancy created throughout the play which must be matched exactly by the appropriate delivery at the highest possible level if the moment is to be properly satisfied and savoured.

'It is the moment when the experienced actor can absorb the concentration of the audience into his own performance.'[19]

It is vital for the Noh performer to be instantly aware of the nature and the mood of his audience so that he is able to adjust his performance to the conditions 'discovered'. This sensitivity must remain during the whole performance in order that he continues to re-appraise these conditions as the performance progresses.

Most of the Noh stories are well known by their audience, and many familiar lines of poetic verse will be quoted in passages of lyrical chant by both Shite and chorus. However, as with the plays of Shakespeare or Aeschylus, the contemporary audience expects to see how the familiar material is represented.

A Noh play of the first rank 'is based on an authentic source, reveals something unusual in aesthetic qualities, has an appropriate climax, and shows Grace'.[20] If the actor chooses to largely ignore the principles upon which all Noh plays are composed then 'any success is out of the question'.[21]

To train a Noh actor means to train his whole body to respond completely and sublimely to the demands of the character and the text. Whereas the grace and strength of the entire attitude of the body carries the overall expression of the chant and the dance, the detail is described by the hands, whether holding and displaying the language of the fan, or not. The feet, similarly, support the detail and manner of the movement of the body. How many western actors act through their feet?!

More simply, an actor has to master five important elements in his art; dancing, chanting and the three types of human form which constitute the basis of role impersonation of age, woman and warriors (usually of considerable strength). If he can manage this, no other method of study will be required. From achieving mastery in these skills the Noh actor will

---

[18] Zeami, F. M. p. 43.   [19] Zeami, F. M. p. 82.
[20] Zeami, F. M. p. 44.   [21] Zeami, F. M. p. 49.

be able to adapt his knowledge to be able to interpret and perform all the characters in Noh.

> *'A real master is one who imitates his teacher well, shows discernment, assimilates his art, absorbs his art into his mind and in his body and so arrives at a level of Perfect Fluency through a mastery of his art... art that achieves Perfect Freedom.'* [22]

> *'If the musical strength of the chant is insufficiently powerful, a dance cannot give rise to any emotive stimulus.'* [23]

One of the most important and complex aspects of Noh is the idea that an actor must present his character according to mood, location and occasion, drawing upon his experience and emotional resources, using highly technical skills within the mask.

Zeami repeatedly discusses this aspect of the Noh actor's art in his treatise, *Mirror Held to The Flower*. He describes this most fundamental of concepts and skills as being the 'Movement beyond Consciousness' and that this skill represents the action of 'the eyes of the spirit looking behind'.

Zeami expounds his theory concisely and neatly in the following way:

> *'The appearance of the actor, seen from the spectator in the seating area, produces a different image than the actor can have of himself. What an actor himself sees, on the other hand, forms his own internal image of himself. He must make still another effort in order to grasp his own internalised outer image, a step possible only through assiduous training. Once he obtains this, the actor and the spectator can share the same image. Only then can it actually be said that an actor has truly grasped the nature of his appearance.'* [24]

Zeami is very certain of how an actor's skills are measured, both by the audience and their fellow actors; it is the ease with which the performance is delivered.

> *'A truly great artist has for many years succeeded in training both his body and his spirit; he can hold back much of his potential in reserve and perform in an easy fashion, so that only seven-tenths of his art is visible. If a beginner tries to perform in this fashion, without the proper practice, he will only imitate what he can observe, and so his spirit and his performance cannot reach beyond that seven-tenths he can grasp. What is more, his own progress will be blocked.'* [25]

There are no short cuts therefore in the training of the Noh actor if he is to achieve the mastery of his art and experience the blooming of the Flower.

---

[22] Zeami, F. M. pp. 66–67.   [23] Zeami, F. M. p. 79.
[24] Zeami, F. M. p. 81.   [25] Zeami, F. M. p. 87.

Holding something in reserve, for the audience, produces a charge of energy and skill which hovers tantalisingly just below the surface. It is a common factor with all great artists and professionals of crafts, that they seem to produce their most exciting work in an atmosphere of relaxed ease and comforting assurance. The audience never sees the work, only the effect of that application of skill and effort.

So Zeami addresses his attention to the student of Noh by pointing towards a level of mastery which is achieved by an understanding of how to hold in reserve a certain amount of their own physical energy, and grasp the principle that 'what is felt by the heart is ten, what appears in movement, seven'.[26] The actor is in fact attempting to attain a performance of 'Perfect Fluency' where there is an absence of tension and effort.

Zeami is never solely preoccupied with the acquisition of technical skills. For the Noh actor...

> 'the essentials of our art lie in the spirit. Real discernment of the nature of the differences between external skill and interior understanding forms the basis of true mastery... he possesses the ability to create for his audience an intensity of pure feeling that goes beyond the workings of the mind'.[27]

To enter into the world of 'Grace' the Noh actor must prepare his body to be able to represent precisely the appearance of a 'deeply beautiful' posture. Once again, Zeami reiterates his thoughts on the disciplines of bodily control, and the time that is given to the development and sustenance of skills.

> 'I cannot repeat too often that an actor must rehearse with the need for the proper preparation of his body always in mind... so that his stance is beautifully assumed representing the true attainment of Grace'.[28]

At this highest level of performance, the actor achieves such a mastery of skill that there are times when he appears to 'do nothing' and these moments are just as engaging for a Noh audience as those which are filled with spectacle and sound. These moments are not written into the scripts like the time 'pauses' of Samuel Beckett or Harold Pinter, yet the actor will instinctively know where they are placed and use them to maximum effect. To do this he can never relax his inner tension or abandon his intense powers of focus.

The actor must rise to a selfless level of art, imbued with a concentration that transcends his own consciousness, so that he can bind together the moments before and after that moment when "nothing happens". Such a process constitutes that inner force that can be termed

---

[26] Zeami, F. M. p. 87.　　[27] Zeami, F. M. pp. 90–91.　　[28] Zeami, F. M. pp. 94–95

"connecting all the arts through one intensity of mind".[29]

Another imponderable 'something in the air' is the state which the Noh actor strives to achieve in his quest for mastery of his art called 'The moment of Peerless Charm'. What Zeami is describing is the aura which can surround the actor during his performance and which may be transmitted to his audience without them necessarily recognising it; its presence felt rather than seen. It is its invisibility which gives it its energy and strength.

> *'An actor will possess this quality precisely because he does not recognise it; if such a moment could in any way be put into words, this charm would no longer exist.'*[30]

In western terms what Zeami is describing is a form of 'stage presence', something which the actor possesses or creates in his performance, which is not scripted or rehearsed, but which has been created some-how by the spirit in which that performance has been prepared and conducted.

In his section on the 'Matter of Mastering the Chant' Zeami continues his theory and practice of absorbing each skill in sequence to such an extent that it should then be deemed forgotten. After the words are learned

> *'forget the voice and understand the shading of the melody. Forget the melody and understand the pitch. Forget the pitch and understand the rhythm... at every stage, the emphasis must be placed on the rhythm... After all these steps are taken, the actor must concentrate on how to bring his performance to flower.'*[31]

In any case the commitment must be total if the actor is to understand the 'Noh with one's very being... he must set aside all other pursuits and truly give his whole soul to our art'.[32]

His lifestyle was and still is monastic by western standards;

> *'sensual pleasures, gambling, heavy drinking represent the Three Prohibitions. Such was the precept of my late father (Kan-Ami). Rehearse with the greatest of effort; do not be overbearing with others.'*[33]

Zeami also endorses the view of his father that at all stages of his development, the Noh actor must continue to maintain the level of skills which he has acquired as well as continually searching for new skills.

> *'To live one's life without ever exhausting the depths of the Noh represents the most profound principle of our school, a principle that must be passed on*

---

[29] Zeami, F. M. p. 97.   [30] Zeami, F. M. p. 99.   [31] Zeami, F. M. p. 103.
[32] Zeami, F. M. p. 105   [33] Zeami, F. M. p. 4.

from child to grandchild generation to generation as a secret teaching of our house.' [34]

In the final stages of his quest for mastery of his art the Noh actor is seeking the state in performance, where all his training has been so absorbed into his inner being, and his physical condition is such that he will have reached the level

'when the actor's unconscious intensity of mind produces spontaneously all effects of performance that can consciously be recognised.' [35]

When this stage has been reached, the actor will represent a state where

'there will seem to be no artistic craft involved, no concern over theatrical effect; rather the actor is able to transmit an emotional state to his audiences that cannot be articulated in words.' [36]

If both the chant and the dance have been fully mastered, then the exquisite appearance of the actor can astonish the heart and the senses of the spectators; and in that instant when they are moved without taking cognizance of their reactions, the Flower of Peerless Charm can be said to exist. Such a moment represents Fascination...

and represents emotional states that transcends the workings of the conscious mind. [37]

Finally the Noh actor must shape his sense of 'ensemble'. Whilst it is he who establishes the pitch of voice, tone and rhythm, once the invocationary drumming and flute calls have preceded his entrance, he must then align himself with the musicians and chorus, and unobtrusively guide the emotional texture and colour of the performance.

'When an actor has achieved a genuine level of Perfect Fluency... no matter which of the myriad roles he may play, [he] will perform with complete ease, indeed even without a conscious sense of ease. his art will surpass skill, transcend intention.' [38]

It is to this ideal state that I think all actors, and all teachers in institutions of acting, should address their energy and their resolve.

_____

[34] Zeami, F. M. p. 109.   [35] Zeami, F. M. pp. 115–116.   [36] Zeam, F. M. p. 118.
[37] Zeami, F. M. p. 134.   [38] Zeami, F. M. p. 136.

INTRODUCTORY NOTES TO

THE DOVE

One of the plays by Zeami which I found deeply moving was *Kinuta* (*The Block*). I considered a detail from the original and began to explore the possibility of designing a play which would unashamedly acknowledge its origins but would be accessible to western audiences.

I used the narrative structure of time and place peculiar to Noh and created a visual, transportable setting which clearly resembled the Noh stage.

I also wanted to write a single character play for a mature woman, and to influence and animate her story-telling techniques through the use of mask and properties.

I knew an actor, Marjorie Solomon, with whom I had worked a number of times before and who, after forty years of performing, still looked for the challenge of something new. She had never performed in mask.

I also persuaded an old friend and highly skilled designer, Liz Walters, to help me with the design of the set and costume and Jack Glover agreed to compose the original music.

The Dove is a tragic love story about a woman Mary, who has been dead for nearly 600 years. In her ghostly state she experiences a sense of loneliness infinitely more profound than the time spent apart from her husband George on earth. In an attempt to cope she recreates daily, in her imagination, the doubts and joys of her relationship with him and her family.

It was first performed at the Old Meeting House Arts Centre in Helmsley North Yorkshire in August 1994, and subsequently toured theatres in Bradford, Birmingham, Richmond, Glasgow and Galway.

THE DOVE

27. Set design for *The Dove*

A 20ft square with a matching sail suspended upstage of it should be stretched out in calico. There is also a calico pathway about a metre wide leading away from the USR corner of the square into the deep, shadowed area surrounding it.

Set DSL of centre is a table with a large luggage basket opened upon it, the lid dangling down the left side. A chair is set beside the right side of the table. On the chair is a red, soft toy cart horse.

Elsewhere on the set are small piles of folded and ironed garments, underwear, a portable rail upstage with a number of items of clothing hanging from it, a small, flat-topped linen basket centre left, and other items which indicate that a journey is being prepared for. An unclad tailor's dummy with head stands USR, apart from the packing.

The important thing is that everything which is packed into the suitcases by the end of the play must be coloured and **everything** *else must be in the colour of the calico, including the Noh garments of the masked Ko-omote Ghost. The final effect should be of a colourless set once the luggage basket is closed.*

The set is open to the audience. A solitary steel spot illuminates the dummy and a tight rectangle of amber illuminates the red horse on the chair.

The lights gradually dim leaving a wide, solitary, steel corridor of light following the pathway up stage, into which glides MARY. She is wearing the Ko-omote Noh mask of a young woman and a less ornate version of the traditional

Noh costume which usually accompanies the mask. She also carries a fan which when opened is blood red.

*The light follows her but **not** with a follow spot. Along the corridor and within the spot she performs a slow sequence of movements with special emphasis on the fan and should transmit to the audience a sense of eager anticipation. This should have a clear sense of ritual, as though it is repeated in a similar way regularly, like a daily prayer.*

She eventually closes the fan, places it ritualistically in the sash at her waist, brings out two claves from a fold in her garment, and strikes them loudly three times before standing stock still, in a stylised listening attitude as though waiting for a reply.

After about seven seconds she strikes them louder with more venom with the same result and gradually falls into an attitude of resignation suggesting that the familiar response of no response prevails.

She turns and glides slowly to the dummy, begins removing her outer garments, ending with the mask, and arranges them carefully upon the dummy as she wore them. Underneath she is wearing comfortable, 'everyday' clothes, a broad leather belt (her granddad's) loosely slung around her waist. She is in her late fifties.

She turns towards the audience, pans across them with a poker gaze, slowly breaks into a smile – almost cheeky. As she does so the steel light disappears and is replaced with straws and amber, upstage, synchronised with and bringing warmth to her smile.

The steel light above dummy and the amber light on the chair which just illuminates both makes us aware of their state – without being obstructive – throughout the play.

MARY: (*Brightly*) I do that every day. Clears this... (*taps her temple*) so that I can remind myself. Otherwise I'll forget. You do don't you?

And there are not many moments that you truly remember. Four or five perhaps, that stick truthfully. The rest pass through and disappear or... change, like... (*Shrugs, can't find the simile. Sits. Still. Then suddenly*) Daft isn't it? Doesn't really make any sense to me either except it works, for me. If I don't do it for any reason I feel uncomfortable, as though I've missed my breakfast.

It isn't that I ever really take them off, my clothes and face I mean. I can't do that really. But I can do this (*referring to the acting space*) in my imagination (*taps her temple*). Forget what I am for a while and get on with this (*moves to table lights move with her*). You see – I'd better be straight with you – I'm a ghost. (*Looks slowly around checking for effect*) Been here before. Actually I've been here more times than I can remember. Been most places come to think of it.

All that, over there (*indicates the Noh Costume*) was over six hundred years ago. Another journey, another land. Someone else. That and me

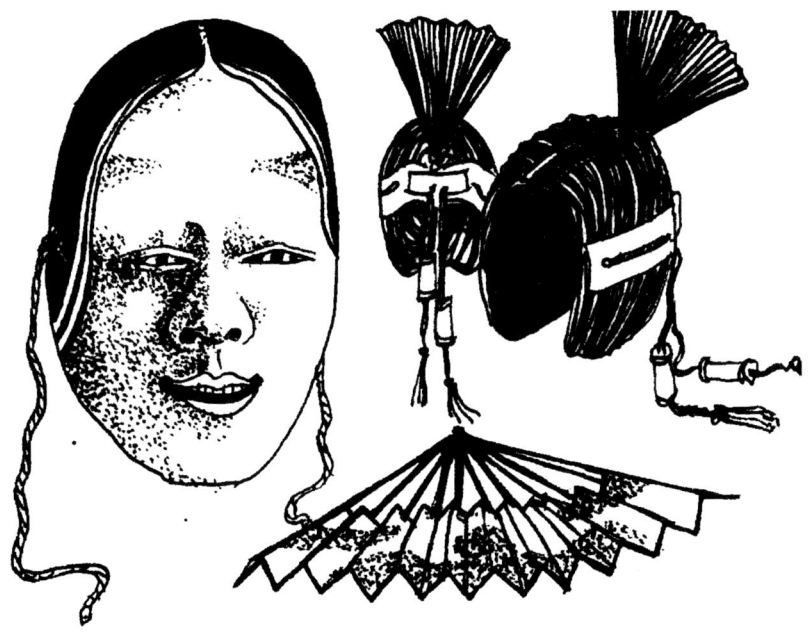

28. Mask, headpiece and fan

29. Prologue sequence

are inseparable, and I can't do anything about it. A reminder of where I've come from – when I became a ghost. And today is another version in another place of the same story. Has to be. Well just look at me and look at me then. Obvious isn't it? I'm older now and I'm somewhere else. Here.

So I'm going to have to keep my wits about me if I'm going to get it right.

She sits down on the chair and picks up a soft toy cart horse and turns it around in her hand teasing out the woollen mane.

Anyway. This is what I do. Sort it out. Search for the familiar clues. This for instance (*refers to the horse*) I've picked this up thousands of times and each time I think something different.

George gave it me. Left it under my pillow just after we were married. I can still feel him after all this time. This (*indicates horse*) I can. In here. (*Taps her temple*) What he represents... my horse.

(*Pause*)

I used to ride him in secret, whenever I could. Seventeen hands of granite with a mouth as soft as chamois and a temperament to match. I could do anything I liked with him. George couldn't. Well he could but he didn't. Too much like hard work for George. Not quick enough either. Nothing was quick enough for George. He was quick enoughfor me.

(*Places it beside the luggage basket on the table in view of the audience*)

I'll leave it 'till last. Tuck it down the sides.

She goes to the portable rail and begins to sift through the clothes. She selects three, drapes two of them over the chair back and starts folding the third garment. She stops, and returns it to the rack and eventually chooses another, returns with it to the table and begins folding it carefully.

Anyway. The worst bit... well, *one* of the worst bits – after I knew he was going away – was going to the boat with him, sitting in the carriage, knowing that it was going to take us right up to the quay. I can't believe how much time we had – to talk in the carriage. A whole journey. We hardly spoke. Seems obvious from this distance. Simple. There was nothing to say.

I knew he had to go, it was the opportunity of a lifetime. But it was in *our* lifetime. Right at the beginning of it. And I couldn't hide my resentment. So I kept quiet.

(*She finishes folding the first garment and places it in the basket. Takes the second garment from the chair and begins folding*)

Say something he said. He kept saying it. Say something. Like what? I said eventually. Anything. Like what? There's nothing to say is there? Think of everything there is to say and it's pointless. Doesn't mean a thing. Waste of time.

And he pulled the lobe of his ear (*Mimics the action slowly*) and looked away. Snap (*clicks fingers*) like that. Well... (*clicks fingers gently so that there is little sound or movement*) more like that.

Mistake, Big mistake. (*Finishes folding the second garment, puts it in the basket and picks up the third garment*) Didn't know what to do you see to get him back because I'd never done that before – snapped at him, and the carriage was rattling on and on and he was looking out of the window not a flicker on and on and I'm thinking that once we'd arrived there'd be nowhere to walk nowhere to be by ourselves just a mess of people doing the same thing, we were late you see. My fault.

(*Pause*)

And that was it. Good-bye. (*Final fold of the third garment before leaving it on the table*) One minute I was there lifting my arm and fluttering my hand like a butterfly (*Begins waving with one hand*) and before I knew it my butterfly was hovering like a Kestrel. (*Hand changes to a talon*) (*Pause*) Silence. (*Pause*) And then (*Taloned hand disappears*) Gone. And from that moment, you know, that until they come back, you're going to lose the feel of them, lose touch. Bad.

(*Pause. Suddenly gets up. Forced brightness*)

Don't know why I do that (*Puts the third garment in the case*) I always come back to that. And time's getting on, and I've all this packing to do.

(*Picks up a jacket shakes it out and begins folding it. Stops, listens, looks slowly around and then fixes on the audience once more*)

The first time I really noticed him – the most stupid thing – he was sitting on a low stone wall with a small boy perched on the end of his knees facing him. I was picking Plum Blossom off the grass that had blown off in the wind and putting it into my frock – I pulled it up at the front. There was a huge spread of it under the trees. I was treading softly so's not to disturb it and I spotted them just a short distance away and he did this

30. Properties

with his jacket.. (*Drapes the jacket around her head like a shawl, arms tossed and crossed like a scarf*)

Stuck his tongue out and started pulling the funniest faces you're over seen. And the little boy was bouncing around all over the place shrieking with laughter. And it wasn't long before I found myself laughing too, out loud.

(*Pause. Removes the jacket from her head*)

And they stopped instantly when they heard me and went off together scuffing across the carpet of petals and over the tumble of rocks to the beach below. Ignored me completely. Shut me out. But I couldn't take my eyes off them. I watched them chasing each other in and out of the sea laughing and splashing. And sometimes one of them would stoop for a moment to look more closely at something they'd spotted (*Crouches down with the jacket folded into a rough rock shape*) and they'd either hunch around it or pick it up and stand together dead still – looking at it – before tossing it aside (*Does so with the jacket*) and playing 'Chase me Charlie' all over again.

(*Stops, listens, looks slowly around smiling, and then fixes on the audience once more*)

I remember thinking then how I'd like to be one of them at that moment even though I knew they didn't want me. So much laughter. Stupid isn't it?

(*Folds up the jacket, places it carefully in the luggage basket*)

And the next time – can't remember the month – was definitely early autumn, and the crop was in and the colours were changing and there was a huge party, everyone was there, the whole village had turned out: I wore this kimono...

(*Describes with her hand the way it was draped across her shoulders*)

given me by my mother. She'd made it herself when she was a young woman. Wanted me to wear it. Said it was time. I *thought* I knew what she meant but I wasn't sure. It was so beautifully... *plain*, the colour of young bamboo. Silk. When you moved slowly it whispered, when you danced it hissed a warning not to.

That night I danced through it. Couldn't help it. And just before we sat down for breakfast, everyone as bright-eyed as when they'd began, I caught sight of him leaning against one of the wooden pillars set in the centre of the earth floor – looking at me. And before I could look away he'd stuck out his tongue and gone through the same sequence he'd performed for the boy on the beach a few months before. He hadn't shut me out you see. He knew I'd watched him all the time. He was like that. I laughed, couldn't help it. Didn't want to help it. And that was it. We were wrapped and folded around each other before our parents had finished their soup. In our heads mind you. Nobody knew. But we were. As quick as that.

(*Pause*)

Six months later, we married.

(*Stops, listens, looks slowly around and then fixes on the audience once more*)

Six months after that he went away. Six hundred years ago. No, five hundred and ninety eight years ago. And those six months, those six months together have all but disappeared. Can hardly remember any of it. Words like... 'passion'. The passion of it. How do you remember the passion of it when you're dead: when you're freezing cold with the dead of it. I'll tell you, you don't. You've all on to remember where you are, in time. That's why I do this. Every day I'm preparing to go to him. Like I did, five hundred and ninety eight years ago.

(Stops, listens, looks slowly around. Picks up a soft textured garment and begins to fold it and then fixes on the audience once more)

And it's when I'm packing like this to go to him that it starts to filter back. What it was like in those few months before we married and the six months after. Because now I can start to feel him again. He's within reach. My body and here *(Taps her temple)* are alive.

(Puts the garment into the basket. Turns behind her searching)

Now...

(Looks around opening and closing little packages and boxes)

where is it? Somewhere obvious I'll bet. How many times do I do that, put something safe where I can see it and then when I want it it's disappeared? Nothing to do with age, I was doing that sort of thing when I was tiny. Mummy used to shake her head. Where did you last put it she'd say. I don't know I'd say. If I knew where I'd put it I'd know where it was wouldn't I?! She never got angry. I never once saw Mummy lose her temper. Well, not with me.

(Pause)

But I can remember her shaking her head. A lot. I think I used to stamp my foot as well. That's what my Dad said. He told me once that I stood in front of him and told him he was a wicked, nasty thing. I was three – so he said – I can't remember. I can't remember a lot of things, unless I touch them. Words vanish so quickly. If I touch things and spend time working with them they stay locked *(Taps her temple)* in here. Same with everyone I should think.

(Looks around again searching, and discovers the belt she's been looking for, slung loosely around her waist)

There it is.

(Removes it and begins to coil it. Stops, listens, looks slowly around and then fixes on the audience once more. Begins to handle the belt unconsciously punctuating the dialogue with it)

Granddad's. Pinched it. Mummy was going to throw it away when he died because it was wide and thick and... ugly. Like Granddad she said. That was a lie for a start. His waist wasn't much bigger than mine. Can tell by the hole *(Indicates)* He was wide, up here *(Indicates her shoulders)* but he was tiny really for a blacksmith. But he could do anything with horses. That's where I get it from. Granddad. He had a way of soothing the fear out of the wildest stallion. Something to do with the way he moved and touched. You never saw him do anything. One minute he'd be humming to himself sorting nails, and the next he'd have a hoof in his lap hammering on a shoe before the horse had time to roll his eyes. I never really know what it was and neither did he, but he was a natural and he encouraged me; gave me confidence with horses. I never saw him ride and yet when I think of him I always see him sitting astride some prancing black cob. Strange.

(*Pause*)

Mummy said he was a bastard. The only time she used that word. A short-arsed bastard, she'd say. And her eyes would fill up with tears. And when I said he was always lovely with me, she'd say you don't know. You don't know half of it. He was ignorant, disgusting she said. He stank of horses and forge and his face was like clinker, she said. I never brought any of my friends home she said. I was ashamed of him. And she was. She ran away to get married so that granddad would have nothing to do with it. She arrived home one day with daddy and carried on as if nothing had happened. Just ignored him. Strange isn't it?

(*She puts the coiled belt into the basket*)

Daddy loved him. Would sit watching him, teasing him for hours. By the forge, on the bench, in the yard, plunging red hot iron, sharpening punches, anywhere.
   They laughed a lot. I used to hear them. In a way they were alike. Quiet, solitary. Unless they were together then they'd be as animated as a pair of clowns. They *looked* like clowns beside each other. Classic. Dad was tall, very tall. (*Indicates great height*) And granddad... well, I told you... (*Indicates granddad's small stature*)

Never saw them together when mummy was around.

(*Stops, listens, looks slowly around, then fixes on the audience once more*)

Daddy used to tell me everything in letters. He used to write beautiful letters. That was another thing about granddad that mummy hated, he was illiterate. That was the thing she hated most of all.

(*Picks up a small rectangular writing case which contains a bundle of letters from George, one from daddy, one from mummy and a fountain pen*)

She gave me this when I went away – the first time.

(She opens the case)

Daddy gave me this.

(Removes a fountain pen)

Mummy didn't want me to be at home. I had to learn she said. Do the things that she'd learned.

All I wanted to do was ride, and stay at home and work on the farm and be with granddad and listen to daddy's stories and... snuggle up to mummy and... I went away.

(Replaces the pen, in the case)

This case was my home, everything I left behind. They're out of fashion now. Nobody writes anymore. *(Puts the writing case beside the basket)*

(Pause)

Every Sunday. Daddy and I used to write to each other chatting nineteen to the dozen, something we rarely did when we were together. Didn't need to somehow. I think he felt guilty about my going away, but he thought it was for the best – so he said. I loathed every last minute of it. It was like a prison cold and separate from anything that was living.

Everything had to be folded and pressed and put in piles the right way into the right drawers or else you'd have to do it over and over until you got it right. It was so pointless and – dulling.

I cried every day at the beginning. They called me a mardy-arse. I told Daddy but all he said was it was for the best, and it never was.

(Returns to writing case and removes daddy's letter)

This was one of my favourite letters from Daddy. I try not to open it too often in case it falls apart. *(Turns it over smiling)* Not bad for six hun... five hundred and ninety-eight years.

(Stops, listens, looks slowly around and then fixes on the letter, opens it and scans bits of it as she refers to it, ending with the postscript)

Every line drew pictures of places and people that I knew – that he knew were special to me. I loved birds and the garden as much as I loved horses and the fields. In this letter, in one sentence, he tells me about a wren's nest that's been tipped out by something and the frantic mother is screaming for her missing fledglings, and in the next there's a picture of a dozing swallow that's appeared for the first time...

(*Turns over the letter*)

... and he talks about some lilies we'd planted together when I was young, and George Davison's new beard and Mummy and... the fact that he was going away – to sort out some troubles in the mountains...

(*Pause. Still. then turns to the postscript*)

And when you thought he'd finished, he'd give me a bit extra – every time.

(*Reading*)

"P.S. As I'm writing this our two favourite doves are strutting and strolling around each other along the wooden guttering of the barn opposite my bedroom window. The sun's warm and brilliant and the pair are all puffedup dipping and tilting their heads cooing as though there's no tomorrow. Framing the barn is a rainbow carrying a butt of rain instead of a crock of gold – again! Never mind. The doves are happy enough. Just thought you'd like to know that."

(*She folds up the letter carefully in the familiar creases puts it in the writing case and gets out mummy's letter.*)

That's the only one I carry about with me of Daddy's, even though I've kept them all.

(*Pause*)

And one of Mummy's. I didn't keep any more of mummy's.

(*The way she fingers the letter reveals her increasing agitation*)

"Make sure you eat properly, keep yourself clean, look after your clothes, and work hard. I was very disappointed to hear that you have been crying again. I can not understand it. You are too old to cry. You are a very lucky girl to be where you are and you will thank me one day. Being away from home is good for you. Teaches you to be strong, etcetera etcetera etcetera... . Granny sends her love, with mine."

(*Smooths out the letter*)

I never liked granny, and she never liked me, so sending her love with granny made me feel as bad as being away from home! Neither granny nor being away from home was good for me! But I still carry it with me.

"P.S. I am making a new dress for the gathering. It is the only thing that keeps me sane in this house when I have got my sewing basket out making or repairing etcetera etcetera etcetera... ."

The rest? (*Refers to the pile of letters*) George.

(*Replaces the letters in the writing case. As she does so she accidentally knocks off a small container of assorted buttons which spill across the table onto the floor, behind the table.*)

Shit!

(*She gets onto her knees and begins collecting them. Sometimes she's invisible*)

I always do that. Every time the whole bloody issue goes everywhere. It's not the picking up that gets me its the fact that I keep knocking it off in the first place – and leave the lid loose. If I didn't leave the lid loose they wouldn't spill. (*Taps her temple*) Obvious.

(*Collects the buttons up putting them on the table brusquely without looking at them, gradually calming*)

Times mummy did that. Not spill them, oh no. Never spill them would mummy, oh no. She'd spread them out in front of her. I loved to see her fingers spreading them, picking them up and looking at them – closely, matching and sorting like jewels. Her fingers were so... careful. They never seemed to get set into anything ugly like they normally were; pinching and picking and clenched. That's when she was most beautiful to me, when she was sorting buttons. (*Begins to put buttons in the tin*)

31. Every button tells a story

She always seemed to be able to find the one she was looking for, or if she couldn't she'd match them so that no one would notice. She had ten times as many as this lot. These are all that's left. I've just used them. For me a button is a button. But not mummy. When her fingers were sifting through them and touching them turning them over so that they were all the same way up she'd sigh or chuckle or tut. There always something she was looking for in here (*Taps her temple*). Each button for mummy was sewn to a story. So there they were, a big, bag, full of stories, each one different. The only time mummy told stories was when she was sifting buttons.

This one for instance came from daddy's uniform.

(*Pause*)

All that was left of it.

(*Drops it in the container. Puts the rest of the buttons in the tin. Picks one out and examines it*)

I wonder... ?

(*She takes the button to one of the garments on the rail next to the dummy, and matches the button she has in her hand with one on the garment. As she does so she becomes aware of the dummy and lets her hand drift down the nearest sleeve-just for a moment, before returning to the table, popping the button into the tin and placing the lid loosely on it.*

She then goes quickly towards the dress rack, stops half way, turns, smiles, returns to the container, secures the lid, puts the tin in the basket, goes back to the rack, chooses the final two coloured dresses from it, places one over the back of the chair and begins folding the other on the table)

The thing I really missed about George was being able to touch him. We're both great touchers me and George. Touch everybody would George. Sometimes got him into trouble.

Kathleen for instance. Lived close by. Took me to oneside at a gathering and said that her John would cut him if he did it again. What? I said. Cut him, she said. Why? I said? Can't tell you she said. Then why start? I said. Finish what you've got to say so that I know what you're talking about I said. I don't know how? she said. Open your mouth and let it come forth. I said. She paused dramatically. He kissed me. she said. Where? I said. Here, she said (*Points to her cheek*) So? I said. Anywhere else? No! – she shrieked. Good God I said he kisses everyone there. Harmless. It's his way. Not my John's way, he didn't like it, she said. Did you? I said. No I didn't but my John went barmy. So Why didn't *he* tell George, I said. He thought it was better coming from me, she said. Scared more like, I thought.

(*Quietly*) Nobody crossed George even though he was the softest man you ever saw.

And I miss him miss him miss him. He's all around me and I miss him. Everywhere I go he's there and I can't bloody touch him. Doesn't matter that I can't see him, it's the touch of him I miss. Here, now! But tomorrow... tomorrow I'm going to him. I'm really going to see him tomorrow and kiss him and cry with him and he'll cup his hand here (*Puts her hand beneath her hairline at the back of her head*) and here (*Cups each elbow in turn*) in there (*Taps her temple*)... and tomorrow, I will – touch him. After all this time. Can't believe it. Frightened to death.

(*Finishes folding the dress quickly and puts it in the basket. Picks up the second dress and holds it against her.*)

This is what I wore, when he left. Bit slack now. But he won't notice. I could be standing here with a child beside me and he wouldn't notice.

(*Pause*)

He'll look straight at me. Tomorrow. (*Laughs*) Big black eyes he's got. Terrifying. Always looks straight at me unless he was angry. Then he'd do this.

(*Turns to the side as she pulls the lobe of her ear*)

Only happened once. No twice. No once. The other time was... nothing. A joke.

(*Pause*)

I've put on this dress so many times I've lost count. I've never *worn* it just put it on, willing him to come home, thinking the dress will do it, bring him back. I know I said that he won't notice but this was where we left off. Anyway...

(*She folds the dress and places it in the centre of the table*)

There. Put it on when I get there. I'll *wear* it!

This is it. The end of it. Nothing leads up to it, it just happens. Cracks out of the air in a way which still surprises me. Here I am looking at this (*Referring to the basket*) knowing the space and what fills it before I even begin...

(*She starts collecting the remaining piles of belongings and begins to put the into the case*)

... and I start packing it. I know you're looking at me and I know what you're looking at and I'm not even thinking about it because I've done it so many times before and as all these little piles fall into place you'll be thinking what will she put in last, last in first out, or if you weren't thinking that you are now that I've suggested it and your mind's going back to time ago (*Picks up the horse*) when I picked this up before and told you oh such a tale of horse and cart that before you know what to think, he's tucked into the side (*Does so*) like that as I promised all seventeen hands of him ago.

(*She takes the writing case from the basket, starts to zip it up, sees the bundle of George's letters, shows them to the audience*)

Lies. All lies. In here (*Taps her temple*) in my imagination. Nothing in this little bundle means anything. It did. Oh yes. Captivating. Opened and folded and fingered and good bits and best bits and heart beats and tremblers and wobblers and... you know what I'm talking about. You've all done it. Written it. Worded it in your own, inimitable style of it. Read it drooled over it, checked it posted waited for it. Lies.

Look.

(*Picks out a letter and shows it to the audience*)

Lies. All lies.

(*Puts the letter back into the pile*)

I'm not going. It's happened before. Twice. Each time I've heard these paper-weak tears of remorse dripping back and each time I've torn them up and prepared for the next time. (*Throws the bundle into the basket*) This time; this time I hear from a grubby little worm of a man who slides up to my door with his grubby little hands wringing his apologies out of his slobber of a mouth. I don't know how to say this he says, but I've been told to tell you that your husband's had to sort out a problem that's turned up unexpectedly – emergency. Very upset he was but there's nothing he can do about it. He says he'll write to you and explain as soon as he can.

You're lying! No he says. Just bringing the message I was told to bring, was paid to bring you; nothing more nothing less. There are rumours but I wouldn't know about them. And he slips round on his grubby little feet and slithers away. Nothing else. Can you believe it?

And here (*Taps her temple*) my imagination is rattling with the gravel of it. I don't know what to think, and there's no way of sorting anything out, of getting any message to him or from him that's the way he works and

32. Packing

that's the way he's always done it and he always gets in touch eventually but eventually this time is too long to have to wait for and I can't be fobbed off with another eventually it's no good. It's no good my darling beautiful man it's no good.

Not this time. Not a scream or a tear in sight. I told you how long we'd been married didn't I – before he went away. Can you believe it? And he's been away so long those six months have almost disappeared, every last love of it.

You've gone George and I can't feel you any more. And if I can't feel you any more then it's no good.

That's at the heart of it. (*Taps her temple*) In here. In my imagination.

(*She unpacks the basket, returning the contents quickly to their original settings.*

She does some of this during the next speech, which she delivers to the audience in a state of calm, even smiling, sometimes showing no trace of sentiment)

And I didn't cut myself or take poison or... anything like that. I just wandered around in fields of tangled, wild grasses and... died.

(When all the stage is set as it was at the beginning she goes to the dummy and starts putting on the overgarments. During this she says the following lines. As she does so the straw and amber lights DS go out)

And I was wrong, about George. He was so preoccupied, he really did have something important to deal with and he couldn't let me go to him. Well he could, but he didn't. That was his choice. Broke my heart. And I couldn't wait.

(Everything is now on except the mask and wig.)

But I can now. All the time in the world.

(She turns to the dummy and puts on the wig and mask with the same ritualistic care as she did when she removed them. As she does so the straw and amber lights are replaced with the steels which began the play)
(She then slowly faces the audience, pans across them for a moment, dips her head to the side as though checking the arrangement of the stage, turns and walks slowly along the pathway)

At the end of the pathway, she turns, listens briefly, and exits.

The stage has returned to the original state of dressing, with the dummy and the chair, as it was at the beginning of the play.

End

INDEX

INDEX